T0287503

Also available at all good book stores

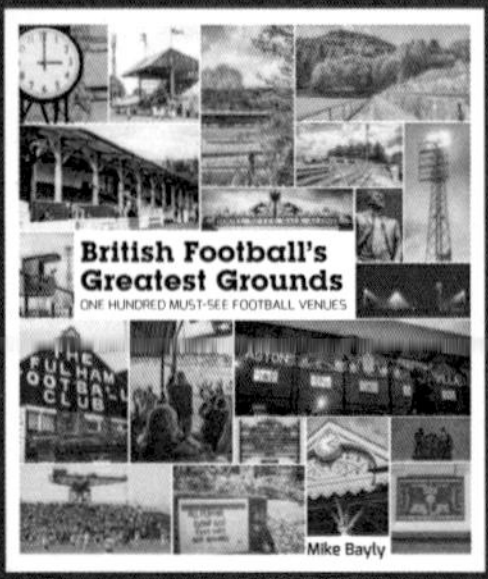

9781785316470

9781785313929

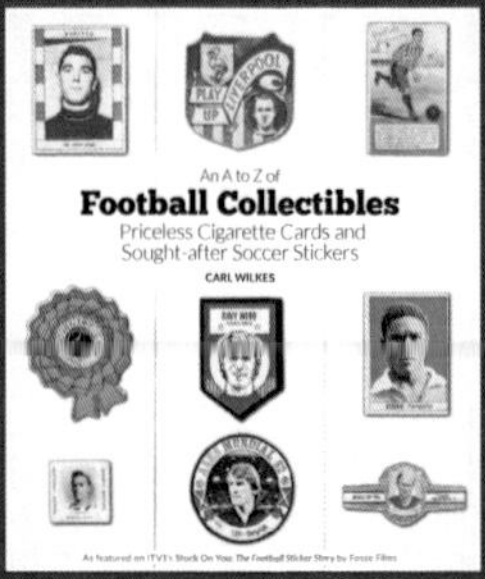

9781785315602

9781785315633

9781785310560

9781909626553

9781908051646

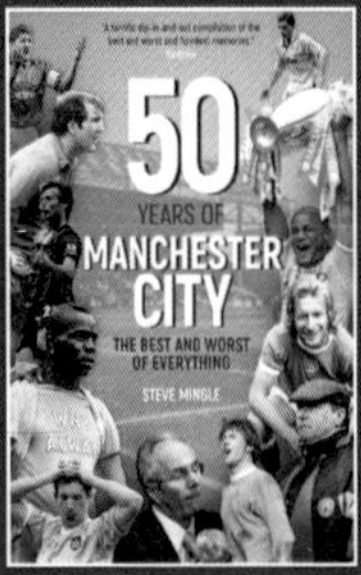

9781785313288

9781909626980

MANCHESTER CITY
MINUTE BY MINUTE

MANCHESTER CITY
MINUTE BY MINUTE

Covering More Than 500 Goals, Penalties, Red Cards and Other Intriguing Facts

DAVID JACKSON

pitch

First published by Pitch Publishing, 2020

Pitch Publishing
A2 Yeoman Gate
Yeoman Way
Worthing
Sussex
BN13 3QZ
www.pitchpublishing.co.uk
info@pitchpublishing.co.uk

© 2020, David Jackson

Every effort has been made to trace the copyright.
Any oversight will be rectified in future editions at the earliest opportunity by the publisher.

All rights reserved. No part of this book may be reproduced, sold or utilised in any form or transmitted in any form or by any means, electronic or mechanical, including photocopying, recording or by any information storage and retrieval system, without prior permission in writing from the Publisher.

A CIP catalogue record is available for this book from the British Library.

ISBN 978 1 78531 667 8

Typesetting and origination by Pitch Publishing

Printed and bound in Great Britain by TJ Books Limited

Contents

Dedicated to the memory of
Neil Davidson and for his wife
Sue and their daughters Bella,
Louisa and Daisy x

Acknowledgements

Manchester City: Minute by Minute was a hard book to research, but thanks to my own memory banks and certain resource outlets, it was made a lot easier.

The goal times are taken from various resources, including BBC match reports, Sky Sports games, *Match of the Day*, the club's official website, endless YouTube highlights (and countless newspaper clippings and old match reports that sometimes tested my eyesight to the limit), plus various other fan sites such as the excellent Sta City and City Till I Die and stats platforms such as Opta, Soccerbase, Transfermarkt and 11v11.

I'd also like to thank City legend Shaun Goater for very kindly providing the foreword for this book. I've been lucky enough to know 'the Goat' and his family for almost 20 years and he has always remained the same, easy-going and friendly guy he was when he was banging goals in for fun for the Blues.

Finally, I'd like to thank Jane Camillin – for green-lighting this series.

Introduction

City fans know this to be true: There really is no other club like Manchester City.

The Blues have been there, done it and bought the T-shirt when it comes to drama. Genuinely, the things that have happened to City sometimes defy belief and no matter how successful the club has become, there are still moments that leave you scratching your head.

Fact: City remain the only club to be relegated as defending top-flight champions.

Fact: City are the only side to score and concede 100 goals or more in one season.

Fact: Denis Law once scored six goals away to Luton only for the referee to abandon the game – Luton won the replay 3-1!

It goes on ... and on ... and on. This is why the phrase 'Typical City' was first coined and the Blues' penchant for last-minute goals is almost unsurpassed. Who else would go into the second minute of added time trailing 2-1 only to score twice in the time that remained to win the Premier League title?

And who else could be 2-0 down in a play-off final with 90 minutes on the clock only to snatch victory from the jaws of defeat? This is just the tip of the iceberg and in the pages that follow, you'll understand why this football club has a habit of putting its fans through the mixer more times than is fathomable.

City should come with a government health warning along the lines of: 'Beware. This football team can seriously damage your health.'

Of course, the fact that life is never dull being a City fan is half the attraction. It's why we love them, no matter how much frustration and angst we invest. And currently, it's the best of times, so enjoy the moment and long may it last.

Now, onwards, and forwards ... the clock is ticking ...

Foreword

By Shaun Goater (1998–2003)

You remember the goal, the moment and the celebration, but the minute you scored in? Not a chance. Of course, if you scored in the first few minutes or last few minutes, you'd have a pretty good idea which minute it was, but for the rest, I have to be honest, I only have a rough idea.

I first met the guy who wrote this book – David Jackson – in Bermuda, maybe 18 years ago. He's from England and is a City fan, but what I liked was that he made me look at the island I had grown up on through different eyes.

Sure we had the ocean and beaches, but he said how much the pure white sands and aqua-blue sea looked like paradise to him. It sounds crazy, but it had just been home before, but it actually made me appreciate Bermuda and its beauty that much more.

The point I'm trying to make is that he is the perfect person to write a book like this, because sometimes you recall a moment, but it's the description that brings everything to life and when you are describing more than 500 different goals, you need to have a good eye for detail!

Back to the minutes issue and my memory!

Though I've seen many of my goals many times on TV or DVD, I didn't take many of the times they were scored in – I know how many I scored and when important milestones were coming up, but I haven't a clue when most of the 103 I scored for City went in timewise.

For instance, I scored my 99th and 100th goals for City in the very last Manchester derby to be played at Maine Road – you couldn't ask for a better way to reach your century, but ask me which minute and I'd probably say that one was in the first half, the second was in the second half!

It turns out the first was on 26 minutes and the second was after 50 – and I am pleased to see they made it into this book! Other memorable goals such as the equaliser away to Blackburn Rovers in 2000, again, I hadn't a clue, but it turns out it was after 60 minutes.

Considering what City went on to do in the years after, I count that as one of my favourites.

The goal time that really surprised me was the one against Wigan Athletic in the 1999 play-off semi-final second leg. I could have sworn it was late in the game that the goal went in – maybe 77 minutes or so – and to the Wigan Athletic fans who still believe it went in off my arm, all I can say is I'm glad VAR wasn't around back then – or VA ARM! Turns out it was 27 minutes, so that's another I completely got wrong.

One I definitely do remember well is the amount of time it took me to score away to Manchester United after coming on as a sub – eight seconds – still a record, I believe (or hope)!

Of course, it's not just about my goals – there are goals that changed the history of the club (I don't need to name them, I'm sure) plus some that you might have enjoyed but have maybe forgotten. That's the beauty of a book like this – it evokes a lot of very happy memories and, as the goals are logged in time order, you can see the patterns over time.

I'll sign off now but enjoy the journey in the pages that follow and when you come across mine, I want you to imagine you can hear the Kippax chanting 'Feed the Goat and he will score!'

I know I will ...

Shaun Goater, Cheshire, August 2020

Minute by Minute...

First half

14 seconds

23 November 2013

City get off to a flying start against Tottenham Hotspur as Jesus Navas scores a spectacular goal from the right of the box. Hugo Lloris's attempt at a clearance only finds Sergio Aguero 25 yards out – his powerful shot is pushed away by the Spurs keeper but Navas is first to the loose ball, clipping a superb angled shot over Lloris and in off the left post to put City 1-0 up.

19 seconds

22 February 2012

Sergio Aguero puts City on the path to a 4-0 home victory over the Europa League holders FC Porto with just 19 seconds on the clock. Yaya Toure plays a pinpoint pass through to the Argentine striker after the Portuguese champions cheaply give possession away with a sloppy pass moments after kicking off. The diminutive front man makes no mistake with his finish as he coolly slots past the hapless Helton in the Porto net. The Blues would go on to win the game 4-0 on the night and 6-1 on aggregate.

24 seconds

29 January 2019

City get off to a dream start away to Newcastle United as Sergio Aguero hooks home a left-foot shot from close range. Raheem Sterling cuts inside on the edge of the box before crossing towards the back post where a stumbling David Silva manages to head back into the middle and Aguero makes no mistake to put the Blues 1-0 up at St James' Park.

30 seconds

1 December 2007

After a piece of had-to-be-seen-to-be-believed defending by Titus Bramble, Geovanni is presented with one of the easiest goals of his career half a minute into the match away to Wigan Athletic. Under no immediate pressure, Bramble manages to completely miss the ball with an attempted clearance, allowing the Brazilian playmaker to steal possession and easily round a furious Chris Kirkland and roll the ball into the empty net to put City 1-0 up.

35 seconds

9 April 2009

Stephen Ireland begins and finishes the move that results in City making the perfect start to their UEFA Cup quarter-final in Germany. His 60-yard pass finds Robinho who easily takes the ball under control. Not content with merely playing the pass, the Irishman breaks forward in an unstoppable run while his Brazilian team-mate skips past two defenders before playing the final killer pass. Without breaking his stride, Ireland knocks the ball into the left-hand corner of the net to put the Blues a goal up after just 35 seconds in the Volksparkstadion. The Ireland/Robinho partnership was one of the most promising aspects of the 2008/09 season and this goal demonstrated their understanding to devastating effect.

40 seconds

7 August 2004

Nicolas Anelka opens the scoring in the Blues' final pre-season game before the 2004/05 season after just 40 seconds, in a man-of-the-match performance. The mercurial Frenchman latches on to Paul Bosvelt's pass before chipping the ball over stranded Lazio goalkeeper Matteo Sereni to send City on the way to a 3-1 victory and Thomas Cook Trophy triumph.

42 seconds

17 December 2005

Christmas comes early for City fans as David Sommeil knocks in a corner after just 42 seconds as the Blues begin to dismantle a poor Birmingham City side from the word go. Jihai Sun's whipped ball into the box is met by the head of Antoine Sibierski who flicks the ball down for his compatriot Sommeil to bury the ball into the net from close range.

45 seconds

22 February 2012

City take a lead inside the first minute against Porto in the Europa League as the Portuguese side lose possession and the ball falls to Yaya Toure who plays a pass into Aguero's path. The City striker runs into the box before a low, right-foot shot into the bottom corner gives the Blues an early lead and the first goal of what will be a comfortable 4-0 win at the Etihad.

1

3 August 1968

With barely a minute on the clock, a youthful Asa Hartford (in the colours of West Brom) plays a poor pass into the middle which Colin Bell easily intercepts and then quickly plays a 40-yard ball into the path of Mike Summerbee on the right flank. Buzzer spots Bobby Owen's intelligent run and plays a superb cross into his path and the former Bury striker deftly places the ball past Osborne in the Baggies' goal to get his City career off to a flying start and put his new club 1-0 up in the FA Charity Shield clash at Maine Road.

2

29 December 2001

Burnley were the surprise package of the 2001/02 campaign and arrived at Maine Road for the final game of the year four points clear of second-placed City at the top of Division One (now Championship). The Blues were under pressure from the chasing pack behind with six clubs within four points in what was proving a highly competitive campaign. City tore into Burnley straight from the kick-off and with just 90 seconds gone Goater found space and crossed a low ball into the six-yard box where Paulo Wanchope slid the ball past Nick Michopoulos and into the net.

26 December 2005

Playing in an advanced position just behind Darius Vassell, Antoine Sibierski is preferred to Andy Cole and justifies manager Stuart Pearce's faith with a fine opening goal away to Wigan Athletic. Escaping the Latics' back line, Sibierski heads past Mike Pollitt less than two minutes after kick-off. City eventually go on to lose 4-3 in a thrilling Boxing Day encounter.

6 November 2008

With the clock reading exactly two minutes as the ball crossed the line, City could not have wished for a better start against Steve McClaren's men in the UEFA Cup Group A game. Shaun Wright-Phillips plays a clever one-two with Jo to beat the Twente back line before placing a low shot past the goalkeeper's right-hand side to give the Blues a 1-0 lead.

21 February 2015

City are awarded a first-minute penalty against Newcastle United at the Etihad after Edin Dzeko is fouled by Anita in the box. By the time the Magpies player had been booked, the game had entered the second minute and Sergio Aguero calmly slots home to make it 1-0 on what will be a long afternoon for Newcastle, who will go on to lose 5-0.

13 September 2017

John Stones scores City's fastest ever Champions League goal as he rises to head David Silva's corner home just a couple of minutes into the group-stage clash with Feyenoord.

3

5 May 1956

Beaten at Wembley in the FA Cup Final just 12 months earlier, City return determined to head back to Manchester with English football's most coveted trophy. And what a start. Don Revie plays an integral role in what is the opening goal for Les McDowall's team against Birmingham City. Revie's 40-yard pass finds Roy Clarke who returns the ball to Revie who then skilfully flicks it into the path of Joe Hayes who slots home the ball with only three minutes on the clock.

28 October 2009

In a trademark burst forward, Stephen Ireland puts the Blues on the way to a 5-1 victory over Scunthorpe United in the Carling Cup just three minutes into the match. Picking up Shaun Wright-Phillips's pass, Ireland takes just two touches to tee up a curling shot from the edge of the area, leaving Scunthorpe keeper Joe Murphy scrambling on the floor as the ball flies past into the back of the net.

26 December 2010

City take the lead with just 73 seconds on the clock at St James' Park in a 2010 Boxing Day clash. An error from Tim Krul presents the ball to Carlos Tevez who plays a superbly weighted ball to Gareth Barry and the former Aston Villa man grabs a rare goal in blue to put City 1-0 up against Newcastle United.

12 December 2011

Many regarded the opening 20 minutes of the game at Stamford Bridge as the finest football the Blues had played during the 2011/12 season. A cool, calm, and collected series of passes between Pablo Zabaleta, Vincent Kompany and David Silva presents the ball to Sergio Aguero with his back to goal just past the halfway line. Kun twists away from his marker before playing a penetrating through ball which sends Mario Balotelli past a stranded Branislav Ivanovic. Although a tackle from the Serbian could easily have resulted in a penalty and a red card, Balotelli stays on his feet to slot past Petr Cech and put City one up in just 98 seconds.

5 November 2013

An historic strike by an historic striker. After David Silva is fouled in the box by a CSKA Moscow defender, the referee points to the spot and Sergio Aguero steps forward to hammer home the resulting penalty to give City an early 1-0 lead while also becoming the Blues' top scorer in European competition at the same time.

25 April 2015

A dreadful error by Aston Villa keeper Brad Guzan gifts City the perfect start at the Etihad. The Villa custodian receives a pass back and looks to knock it across the box to his full-back – but gets it horribly wrong and the advanced Sergio Aguero collects the loose ball and rolls it into the empty net for one of his easiest goals yet for City.

11 March 2017

David Silva grabs a crucial early goal as City look to book a place in the FA Cup semi-finals. Playing relegation-threatened Middlesbrough at the Riverside Stadium, Boro allow Pablo Zabaleta too much time and space to send a precision cross into the six-yard box where Silva prods home to make it 1-0.

4

3 April 2010

Emmanuel Adebayor begins an extraordinary start for City away to Burnley. The Togolese striker collects a corner from the left on the volley before drilling a low shot past the keeper and two defenders on the line from ten yards to get the Blues off to a flyer at Turf Moor.

30 September 2014

A further penalty to add to his collection, Sergio Aguero chases a cross into the box and is pulled back by former City defender Maicon. The referee spots the infringement and Aguero converts the penalty to give the Blues an early lead in the Champions League group-stage clash with AS Roma at the Etihad.

10 May 2015

Not the prettiest of goals, but another strike for Sergio Aguero against QPR. This one is made and finished by Aguero who runs at the QPR defence and despite the presence of four defenders, he bundles through them all and sees the ball bounce kindly enough to lift it over the keeper and give City an early 1-0 lead.

13 August 2016

When Raheem Sterling is fouled in the box, there's only one man who is going to step up and finish the job off and that man, of course, is Sergio Aguero, who plants a powerful penalty kick high to the keeper's left to put City 1-0 up just four minutes into Pep Guardiola's Premier League reign.

5

3 August 1968

City's rip-roaring start to the FA Charity Shield clash with West Brom just gets better as the Blues double their lead with only five minutes on the clock. With Colin Bell dominating the early exchanges, he sprays the ball out to Mike Summerbee whose tempting cross is nodded into his own goal by Graham Lovett to put City 2-0 up in the game played at Maine Road and Buzzer claims his second assist of the afternoon despite the match having just begun a few minutes before.

8 January 1988

This was a special FA Cup third-round tie for many reasons, but the main one was the fact City had beaten Huddersfield Town 10-1 in the league just eight weeks earlier. The hosts and their supporters see this as an ideal opportunity for revenge but the Blues, backed by more than 7,000 travelling fans at Leeds Road, are in no mood for charity and when Ian Brightwell puts City 1-0 up after just five minutes, the hosts must fear another drubbing – but there is no further scoring in the first half with City going in at the break a goal to the good.

9 November 2003

City draw first blood in the last ever Manchester derby as Kevin Keegan's side score with their first attack. Nicolas Anelka dispossesses Rio Ferdinand and sets up a chance for Shaun Goater who shoots and appears to catch Fabien Barthez by surprise. The French goalkeeper spills the half-hit shot into the path of Anelka, makes no mistake from close range and gives City a 1-0 lead.

3 April 2010

City make it two goals in two minutes to go 2-0 up against Burnley. With the Clarets still reeling from Emmanuel Adebayor's fourth-minute strike, Carlos Tevez plays a clever pass into the feet of Craig Bellamy who checks inside one challenge before rolling a low shot past the keeper to double the Blues' lead at Turf Moor.

26 December 2010

Carlos Tevez doubles City's lead at St James' Park with a second goal inside five minutes against Newcastle United. Tevez, who set up Gareth Barry's opener on two minutes, rifles a shot into the top of the net with his left foot after sprinting on to a fine James Milner cross to give the Blues a quickfire 2-0 lead.

6 October 2012

A typical Aleks Kolarov strike, full of quality and venom. When City are awarded an early free kick at home to Sunderland, the Serbia left-back curls the ball past the wall and into the roof of the net before the Sunderland keeper has even seen it – a spectacular effort that puts City 1-0 up.

17 February 2013

A great team goal involving David Silva, Carlos Tevez and Yaya Toure. Yaya and Silva exchange passes in midfield before the Ivorian midfielder finds Tevez on the edge of the area – Tevez clips a ball back into Yaya's path as he drives into the box and he collects the pass, feigning to shoot before taking the ball round the keeper and slotting home to give the Blues an early lead against Leeds United in the FA Cup fifth-round tie at the Etihad.

2 April 2017

City get off to a great start away to Arsenal as Leroy Sane puts the Blues 1-0 up at the Emirates Stadium. The Gunners are all at sea as Kevin De Bruyne finds Sane who then uses his electric pace to outrun a defender and take the ball around keeper David Ospina before sending an angled shot just beyond the desperate dives of two Arsenal defenders and into the empty net.

6

11 April 2012

With City and United both in action in midweek, the Blues need to keep winning games and hope the Reds slip up in a thrilling all-Manchester title race. Sergio Aguero ensures this game gets off to a flying start as he picks the ball up just inside his own half and skips past a couple of challenges before lashing a 25-yard shot past Ben Foster to put the Blues in front.

7

3 April 2010

City's blistering start at Turf Moor just gets better as Carlos Tevez scores the Blues' third inside seven minutes. When Emmanuel Adebayor fires a low shot on goal, Burnley keeper Brian Jensen spills a relatively easy save into the path of Tevez who is on hand to tap the ball home – his 20th goal of the campaign – and all but wrap up the points with only seven minutes played. Incredible stuff.

27 September 2014

Another fox-in-the-box goal for Sergio Aguero. A corner from the left is swung across and Pablo Zabaleta climbs highest on the edge of the box to head the ball down to Aguero, who spins on the edge of the six-yard box and rasps a shot into the corner of the net to give the keeper no chance as City go 1-0 up away to Hull City.

8

4 December 2015

City score an early goal at Old Trafford to go 1-0 up against Manchester United. James Milner finds David Silva's run into the box with a neat pass and the Spaniard reaches the byline before firing a low cross into the six-yard box for Sergio Aguero to sweep home.

8 May 2016

Fernandinho's cushioned header finds Sergio Aguero on the edge of the Arsenal box – the Argentinian star spins away from his marker before firing a powerful left-foot shot in from just inside the 18-yard line to give City a 1-0 lead over Arsenal at the Etihad.

14 September 2016

The first of yet another Sergio Aguero hat-trick comes in this Champions League group-stage clash with Bundesliga side Borussia Monchengladbach in a game hastily rearranged from the previous evening after torrential rain made the surface unplayable. Aleks Kolarov's superb low cross from the left is turned in at the near post by the prolific Argentine to give City a 1-0 lead at the Etihad.

9

26 December 1981

Asa Hartford, having already had a goal harshly ruled out, makes no mistake when he is given a second chance soon after. Ray Ranson plays a ball down the right flank for Kevin Reeves to chase and his low cross only finds Phil Thompson – but Hartford nips in, taking the ball off the Liverpool defender before turning quickly and firing a low shot into the bottom left-hand corner of the net to put City 1-0 up at Anfield.

23 March 1988

In a game ridiculed by many and a competition overlooked by some, City take the lead in the 1988 Full Members' Cup Final at Wembley. City were taking on Chelsea and a crowd of 67,236 had made a mockery of those who had discarded the cup as unimportant and Steve Kinsey fires home from close range to give the Blues a flying start.

22 September 2015

Sergio Aguero thumps home another penalty after Jesus Navas had been fouled in the box to put the Blues on the way to a comprehensive 4-1 League Cup win at the Stadium of Light.

23 January 2016

Despite falling behind after just 53 seconds, away to West Ham United, City respond quickly to level the scores. After being fouled in the box, Sergio Aguero steps up to send the keeper the wrong way to make it 1-1 at Upton Park.

24 September 2016

Fernandinho plays the ball to the right flank for Bacary Sagna, and the former Arsenal man hits a low cross in towards Sergio Aguero who moves past a defender with his first touch then fires a low shot through the legs of Swansea keeper Lukasz Fabianski from the corner of the six-yard box to give City an early 1-0 lead at the Liberty Stadium.

7 August 2020

City's high press pays dividends in the Champions League round of 16 second-leg clash with Real Madrid. Raphael Varane dithers in possession to the right of his own six-yard box. Gabriel Jesus nicks the ball off his toes and passes to the unmarked Raheem Sterling who rolls the ball into the net despite a despairing lunge from a Militao. It is Sterling's 100th goal for the club and what a prestigious fixture to get it in.

10

11 May 1985

City need victory in the final game of the 1984/85 season to claim the last Division Two promotion berth. A crowd of more than 47,000 pack Maine Road to hopefully see the Blues win a place back in the top flight and Billy McNeill's side get the start they are looking for when Jim Melrose releases 18-year-old winger Paul Simpson down the left flank and he accelerates past two defenders before delivering a precision low cross that David Phillips side-foots home from five yards. It is Phillips's 11th goal of the season and it sparks a mini pitch invasion as a result.

3 January 2012

Sergio Aguero starts the New Year as he finished the old one – in red-hot form. Collecting a short pass from David Silva, Aguero nudges the ball forward before rifling in a shot from 22 yards out that bounces just in front of Liverpool keeper Pepe Reina and then underneath the Spaniard's despairing dive to put City ahead at the Etihad.

4 February 2012

As Manchester is gripped by blizzard conditions, so City sweep Fulham away with a bright and breezy start.

The Blues are ahead after just ten minutes as Sergio Aguero bags only his second penalty for the club after sending Mark Schwarzer the wrong way from the spot as City go on to win 3-0 at the Etihad.

15 December 2012

City go in front against Newcastle United at St James' Park with only ten minutes played with an incisive move that begins with Yaya Toure's through ball to Samir Nasri, and the Frenchman's unselfish side pass to Sergio Aguero gives the Argentina striker an easy chance to convert from seven yards out.

7 December 2013

An early goal puts City ahead at the Etihad. A good run and cross by Aleks Kolarov sees the Serbian left-back fizz a low ball towards the penalty spot where Sergio Aguero is waiting to lash home with a left-foot shot that gives the Southampton keeper no chance.

24 April 2014

After seeing his prolific season interrupted by a hamstring injury, this was Sergio Aguero's first goal for almost three months – and what a way to return to scoring. He wriggles away from one challenge before lashing a shot from 25 yards out to put City 2-0 up on a day when fellow Argentines Pablo Zabaleta and Martin Demichelis will also score.

13 September 2017

A great burst down the right flank by Kyle Walker sees the England defender spot Sergio Aguero's run towards the six-yard box, and his low cross is turned in expertly from close range by the Argentine to put City 2-0 up away to Feyenoord in the opening Champions League group-stage clash.

11

28 February 1976

Peter Barnes puts City ahead in the League Cup Final against Newcastle United with just 11 minutes on the clock. Asa Hartford floats a ball towards skipper Mike Doyle on the left of the Magpies penalty area and he rises to nod into the six-yard box, causing a scramble that sees the ball fall to 19-year-old left-winger Barnes, who prods home from a few yards out before running to the City fans banked behind the goal.

14 May 1981

A goal that has largely been forgotten over the years, mainly thanks to the goal that was scored by Tottenham's Ricky Villa later in the same game. Nobody, however, could deny the fact that City's teenage midfielder Steve Mackenzie volleyed home one of the best goals ever seen at Wembley. City had gone behind to an early Steve Archibald goal when the ball is cleared only as far as Tommy Hutchison on the edge of the Spurs box – Hutch cushions a header into Mackenzie's path and the teenage midfielder strikes a perfect right-foot volley from just outside the box into the top-left corner of the net. Mackenzie's sumptuous strike deserved a better fate than being consigned to the 'losers' goals archive.

23 September 1989

City, just promoted and back amongst the nation's elite, began the 111th Manchester derby having won only one match of the new campaign. But it would soon turn into a day of joy for the City fans, who hadn't tasted derby victory for 13 long years. After the game was delayed for crowd trouble in the North Stand it was the Blues who came out more focused and, on 11 minutes, went ahead. Andy Hinchcliffe sprays a fine cross field pass to David White who controls and sends in a low angled cross into the box – it is misjudged by Manchester United's Gary Pallister who had gone towards the near post too soon, leaving David Oldfield free to thump the ball past Jim Leighton and send Maine Road wild.

16 October 2004

Given the recent history between City and Chelsea, this game was expected to be nothing more than a formality. Not only had Chelsea finished runners-up the season before as City had been battling to avoid relegation, but the London club had beaten the Blues in nine of the two sides' previous ten meetings. However, City are in no mood to roll over against the unbeaten Premier League leaders. Paul Bosvelt pounces on a loose ball after William Gallas slips in possession and the Dutch midfielder launches a long ball to Nicolas Anelka who manages to steal in front of last defender Paulo Ferreira, who clumsily brings the City striker down in the area. The referee awards a spot kick and Anelka confidently strokes in the penalty as Chelsea concede their first league goal away from home that season and only their second of the campaign. It also gives City a 1-0 win and ends Chelsea's unbeaten start.

4 December 2013

A lovely move starts with Edin Dzeko playing a clever ball inside the full-back for Pablo Zabaleta to run on to. The City defender then spots Sergio Aguero in the box and plays a low cross in at pace and Aguero fires home from close range for a goal made in Argentina – and to give the Blues a 1-0 lead away to West Bromwich Albion.

12

29 April 1970

Neil Young puts City 1-0 up in the European Cup Winners' Cup Final against Polish side Gornik Zabrze. As torrential rain soaks all inside the Prater Stadium in Austria, Francis Lee cuts in from the left wing, escapes a tackle from Alfred Olek, and strikes a fierce shot that keeper Hubert Kostka parries and Young makes no mistake, tucking the loose ball home from close range.

4 August 2019

City get the upper hand in the 2019 Community Shield against Liverpool at Wembley. In a bid to get an early psychological advantage for the season ahead, the Blues edge ahead when Kevin De Bruyne's cross is flicked on by David Silva for Raheem Sterling who manages to get a slight connection under keeper Alisson and there is just enough power for the ball to cross the line.

13

7 November 1987

What was the start of a quite incredible afternoon at Maine Road begins as City take a 1-0 lead over Huddersfield Town. The visitors, managed by Newcastle United legend Malcolm Macdonald, should have been three goals up by the time Neil McNab picked up the ball midway inside the Terriers' half, cut inside and drilled a low left-foot drive into the bottom-right corner of the net.

23 September 1989

With City still celebrating the opening goal against Manchester United, the Blues double their lead to lift the roof off Maine Road. Mal Donaghy dithers on the edge of his own box and Trevor Morley steals the ball, firing in a low shot that keeper Jim Leighton pushes out. Paul Lake picks up the loose ball, goes around a defender and fires in a shot that Leighton again saves, but this time Morley is first to react and he forces the ball home from a couple of yards out to put City 2-0 up.

13 September 2008

His signing had shocked the world and for 12 months his performances would delight the City faithful. It was easy to overlook the significance of Robinho's arrival on the day that the Blues were taken over by Sheikh

Mansour, but for City fans, the Brazilian's arrival was a true mark of things to come. Ironically, his debut would come against Chelsea – a side he had been heavily linked with ahead of his move to the Etihad – and it takes just 13 minutes for the British record transfer to prove worthy of the £32m outlay as he announces his arrival with a precision free kick that takes a slight deflection on its way past Petr Cech to send the City fans wild and put his new team 1-0 up.

10 September 2011

David Silva receives the ball on the left of the Wigan Athletic box and feigns a shot before looking up to see Sergio Aguero darting into the box. Kun takes the ball a touch to the right before hitting a low drive through the legs of a Wigan defender and into the bottom left-hand corner of the net to put City 1-0 up against the Latics.

18 September 2011

Gareth Barry passes to David Silva on the edge of the Fulham box and the Spanish playmaker plays the ball through to Sergio Aguero who darts clear of his marker before drawing Mark Schwarzer off his line and lifting the ball over the keeper and into the corner of the net to give City a 1-0 lead at Craven Cottage.

18 October 2014

The first of four goals for Sergio Aguero against Spurs. Frank Lampard plays a simple pass to Aguero in the box and, after sizing up his options, he cuts back inside before hitting a low shot across the keeper and into the far corner to give the Blues an early lead.

5 August 2018

Sergio Aguero scores his 200th Manchester City goal to put City 1-0 up in the 2018 Community Shield clash against Chelsea at Wembley. The Blues open the scoring when Phil Foden bursts down the middle before playing a side pass to Aguero on the edge of the Chelsea box – he allows the ball to move across his body before firing a crisp low drive into the bottom-right corner of the net to give Willy Caballero no chance.

14

14 December 2013

Sergio Aguero's prolific December continues with a stunning volley to give City the lead against Arsenal in what will be a nine-goal thriller. Samir Nasri's corner is glanced towards the far post by defender Martin Demichelis and waiting to finish from close range is Aguero, who spectacularly volleys home with the outside of his right boot.

19 April 2016

This goal is all about the delivery, with Aleks Kolarov providing a precise, whipped-in cross for Sergio Aguero to leap and guide a header into the net for a superb goal against Newcastle United. It puts City 1-0 up at St James' Park, though the Magpies will equalise later in the half to earn a 1-1 draw.

15

11 May 1985

City double their lead against Charlton Athletic and Paul Simpson is once again the provider. The young left-winger sends a cross into the six-yard box where Andy May leaps to meet it and sends a looping header into the top left-hand corner of the net in a must-win game for the promotion-chasing Blues.

17 February 2013

Another penalty dispatched by Sergio Aguero as City go 2-0 up in quick time against Championship side Leeds United in the FA Cup. It is Aguero himself who is fouled in the box and the Argentine delivers maximum punishment from the spot with a customary cool finish to give the Blues a foot in the sixth round with only a quarter of an hour played.

29 January 2014

Sergio Aguero's seventh goal in 14 days comes as David Silva spots his run into the Spurs box, plays a simple pass into his path and, as Hugo Lloris comes out to the corner of the six-yard box, Aguero casually slips a delightful angled shot into the opposite corner. A classy finish from a striker at the top of his game. It is also the opening goal of a stunning 5-1 win at White Hart Lane for the Blues.

24 February 2016

A static Dynamo Kyiv defence is punished as City take an early lead in the first leg of the Champions League round of 16 tie in Ukraine. Yaya Toure heads down a cross to Sergio Aguero who has time to tee up a shot, before firing past the home keeper to set the Blues on their way to a priceless 3-1 victory.

10 September 2016

Kevin De Bruyne takes a gamble as a long ball is played into the Manchester United half – and it pays off as Kelechi Iheanacho gets a glancing header on the ball to set the Belgian through on goal – De Bruyne races towards the United box before giving David De Gea 'the eyes' and looking at one corner and firing it in the opposite side to put City 1-0 up at Old Trafford.

16

22 October 1994

In what will become a Premier League classic, City strike the first blow against Spurs at Maine Road as a right-wing cross is half cut out by a young Sol Campbell, but, as the defender loses his bearings, Paul Walsh nips in and tucks the ball away low to keeper Ian Walker's left-hand side to give the Blues a 1-0 lead.

24 February 1996

An epic clash between City and Newcastle United sparks into life at Maine Road. City, struggling near the foot of the table against Kevin Keegan's title-chasing Magpies, start the better of the two success-starved giants and deservedly take the lead when Scott Hiley makes an impressive run down the wing and cuts the ball back to Nigel Clough whose vicious low drive clips Niall Quinn's heel and the ball spins agonisingly over the stranded Pavel Srnicek. There is a moment's silence and then a deafening roar as the ball nestles in the back of the net sending the packed Maine Road wild with delight.

22 September 2013

What a way for City's No.16 Sergio Aguero to bring up his 50th goal – and it had to be in the 16th minute of course! Samir Nasri's clever pass to the overlapping Aleks Kolarov sees the Serbian power the ball into the six-yard box where Aguero reacts in an instant, hooking a left-foot volley past David De Gea to put the Blues on the way to another Manchester derby win. Clinical, instinctive and sublime – this landmark strike had everything.

19 October 2013

Fernandinho's pass to Alvaro Negredo sees the Spaniard leave the ball for Sergio Aguero who bursts through the West Ham defence, draws the keeper off his line and then tucks the ball into the bottom left-hand corner to give City a 1-0 lead against West Ham United at Upton Park.

2 February 2016

A low cross by Jesus Navas finds Sergio Aguero eight yards from goal and, after moving past the defender with his left foot, he then pokes it high over the keeper and into the corner of the net with his right to make it 1-0 against Sunderland at the Stadium of Light. It will prove to be the game's only goal.

17

7 January 2020

Pep Guardiola's decision to take on Manchester United in the first leg of the Carabao Cup semi-final without a recognised striker quickly ties the Reds in knots. Led by the twin false nines of Bernardo and De Bruyne, City swarm over Ole Gunnar Solskjaer's side and dictate proceedings before finally breaking the deadlock. The Blues' opener comes from Portuguese schemer Bernardo with a goal worthy of the occasion. Collecting Kyle Walker's square pass some 30 yards from goal, Bernardo checks inside on the edge of the Reds' box before unleashing an unstoppable drive into the top-left corner via the underside of the crossbar. A stunning strike to put City 1-0 up.

18

9 January 2016

Simply stunning. Sergio Aguero collects a back-heeled pass 30 yards from goal before jinking past two defenders in the blink of an eye, then sells another a dummy as he enters the box and plants the ball past the goalkeeper all within the space of six blistering seconds to put City 1-0 up in the FA Cup third round away to Norwich.

3 January 2019

A quite incredible clearance by John Stones proves to be one of the crucial moments of the 2018/19 Premier League title race. Sadio Mane races into the City box, slides a low shot past Ederson and on to the foot of the post but as John Stones fires his clearance at Ederson, the ball hits the City keeper and rebounds towards the net where Stones desperately lunges to clear. The goal-line technology suggests 1.12 centimetres of the ball didn't cross the line – so it is no goal and the score remains 0-0.

19

2 April 2016

A rampant City go three goals up within the first 20 minutes against Bournemouth at the Vitality Stadium. Jesus Navas whips a high cross into the six-yard box that Sergio Aguero leaps for and his header creeps over the line, despite the defender's desperate attempt at a clearance, to compound the Cherries.

9 April 2016

Though a penalty, this is a landmark goal for Sergio Aguero, who enters the Blues' all-time top ten goalscorers list with his 130th strike for the club, as well as celebrating his 200th appearance for City. The penalty is awarded for a foul on Aleks Kolarov and comfortably dispatched by Aguero to make the score 1-1 against West Brom at the Etihad.

16 April 2016

The start of a memorable afternoon for Sergio Aguero away to Chelsea. Some 20 yards out, Aguero pushes the ball to his right and past a defender before hitting a low shot into the bottom right-hand corner with unerring accuracy and power to give City a 1-0 lead at Stamford Bridge.

29 October 2016

After failing to win the previous three games, City return to form at The Hawthorns and it is a well-constructed goal that puts the Blues on the way to a thumping 4-0 win over West Bromwich Albion. Ilkay Gundogan powers towards the hosts' box before playing a pass into Sergio Aguero's darting run, and the City striker makes no mistake with a powerful low drive past the keeper from the right.

20

3 April 2010

Patrick Vieira's first goal in City colours gives the Blues a 4-0 lead at Turf Moor. The former Arsenal man powers a header from a left-wing corner past the keeper to make it 4-0 against Burnley as Roberto Mancini's side run riot.

5 November 2013

Another goal for the prolific Sergio Aguero out of nothing. Samir Nasri's arrowed pass finds Aguero in the box with his back to goal – he spins away from his marker and fires into the bottom right-hand corner with a shot across the keeper to double the Blues' lead over CSKA Moscow on the night with only 20 minutes of the Champions League group-stage clash played.

18 October 2014

Christian Eriksen had levelled for Spurs just two minutes after Sergio Aguero's opening goal but City were soon back in front. James Milner plays a short pass into the path of Frank Lampard who is nudged in the back as he is about to collect the ball and the referee awards a spot kick that Aguero comfortably dispatches for his second of the afternoon.

1 March 2020

City take the lead at Wembley in the Carabao Cup Final against Aston Villa. After dominating the early stages, the Blues make the breakthrough when Rodrigo's teasing cross is nodded back across the box by Phil Foden, and Sergio Aguero puts the ball home from close range.

21

25 November 2014

Taking on Bayern Munich in a must-win Champions League group-stage clash at the Etihad, Sergio Aguero is dragged down in the box by Medhi Benatia as he is about to pull the trigger and the referee awards a penalty – and sends the Bayern defender for an early bath. Aguero makes no mistake from the spot with a right-footed effort to put City 1-0 up on what will be an unforgettable night for City's talismanic striker.

3 December 2014

Having fallen behind to a goal from Sunderland at the Stadium of Light just two minutes earlier, Sergio Aguero rides one challenge outside the box before hitting a powerful shot past the Black Cats' keeper from just inside the box to make it 1-1.

26 August 2017

City quickly level the score at the Vitality Stadium after Bournemouth had gone ahead through a Charlie Daniels howitzer. There seems little on as David Silva looks up but the gifted Spaniard threads the perfect pass to Gabriel Jesus who races on to the edge of the box before sending a low shot into the bottom-right corner of the net from 15 yards out.

11 July 2020

Riyad Mahrez plays a clever lofted pass to Gabriel Jesus outside the Brighton box and the Brazilian's header finds Raheem Sterling who cuts inside of one challenge before arrowing a low shot into the bottom-right corner of the net from 18 yards out. It was Sterling's 25th of the campaign – equalling his personal best for a season – and further cemented his position as leading scorer for the club during the 2019/20 campaign.

22

23 October 2011

One of City's most famous goals and the first of what will be an unforgettable Manchester derby at Old Trafford. David Silva probes the United defence before feeding the overlapping James Milner to his left – Milner's low precision cross into the box finds Mario Balotelli on the edge of the box and the Italian guides a superb low drive into the bottom-left corner of the net and just inside the post to put City 1-0 up over Manchester United. Balotelli immediately pulls up his shirt to reveal the message 'Why always me?' Genius.

6 November 2012

With City on the ropes against Ajax and watching their Champions League campaign unfold before their eyes, it is Yaya Toure who decides to take the game by the scruff of the neck and lead by example. Trailing 2-0 to the Dutch giants with only 17 minutes played, City cannot afford to lose this game and, as a cross comes in from the right, Yaya controls the ball at the back post and swivels all in one movement to bury the ball past the Ajax keeper and bring City back into the game at 1-2 to Ajax.

19 August 2013

It takes Sergio Aguero just 22 minutes of Manuel Pellegrini's reign to find the back of the net as City start the 2013/14 campaign in rip-roaring fashion. Aguero collects the ball in midfield before turning on the afterburners and heading towards the Newcastle United box. He then fires a low shot into the bottom left-hand corner from 20 yards – a terrific way to start the new season.

3 May 2014

A crucial goal and one that puts City back on course for a second Premier League title in three years. Sergio Aguero darts forward into the Everton box and fires a fierce low shot past Tim Howard to level the scores after the Blues had fallen behind on 11 minutes. It would be Sergio's last act of the afternoon as he then limps off with a groin injury – he'd only returned after a three-month lay-off ten days earlier. Despite the blow, City go on to win 3-2 and climb to the top of the table with just two games remaining. It's his 28th goal of another stunning – though injury-interrupted – season.

23

23 April 1904

The goal that settles the 1904 FA Cup Final and secures Manchester City's first major trophy comes after 23 minutes of the game against Bolton Wanderers played at Crystal Palace in London. George Livingstone's right-wing pass eludes Bolton's Archie Freebairn and reaches Billy Meredith, who dribbles beyond Bob Struthers for a run on goal. The Welsh winger shoots to goalkeeper Davies's left, scoring the opening goal. Suspicions of offside are unfounded and City go on to win the game courtesy of Meredith's strike.

21 May 2017

The first of two goals for Sergio Aguero at Vicarage Road comes after a measured through ball from Kevin De Bruyne sets Kun clear, and his low shot to the left of the keeper doubles the lead for the Blues on the final day of the 2016/17 campaign.

24

26 April 1969

City take on Leicester City in the 1969 FA Cup Final at Wembley with the Blues looking for a first success in the competition for 13 years. What will prove to be the only goal of the game comes when Mike Summerbee skips down the right flank before crossing low into the Leicester box where Neil Young arrives with perfect timing to thump a powerful rising shot past Peter Shilton and give City a 1-0 lead. It will be enough to secure the trophy for Joe Mercer's men who were still defending league champions at the time.

21 January 2014

With City already 6-0 up against West Ham United after the League Cup semi-final first leg, this was always going to be a comfortable night for the Blues at Upton Park and Sergio Aguero's goal is the result of yet more bad marking by Sam Allardyce's side. Marcos Lopes flicks the ball to Aguero who just about keeps possession before nudging it past a defender and tucking home with ease via a clever chip past the keeper and putting City 2-0 up on the night and 8-0 ahead on aggregate.

9 September 2017

Another home goal against Liverpool for Sergio Aguero – his sixth in succession against the Reds at the Etihad – equalling the Premier League record for successive goals in a fixture. From just inside the Liverpool half, Kevin De Bruyne plays a sumptuous pass that splits the Reds' defence apart for Aguero to race on to. He rounds keeper Simon Mignolet before slotting the ball into the empty net to put City on the way to a memorable afternoon against the Merseysiders.

25

13 September 2017

Gabriel Jesus continues City's blistering start as he fires home from close range to put the Blues 3-0 up away to Feyenoord in the opening Champions League group-stage clash in Holland. The Dutch side are simply overwhelmed by Pep Guardiola's side and, with more than an hour still to play, aware that they could be on the end of a cricket score if the game continues as it has started.

2 July 2020

The title race might have been over, but City were still keen to show Liverpool that to be the best, you must beat the best. The Merseysiders had just been crowned Premier League champions, but City still had a point to prove and boy, would they do it. On 24 minutes, Raheem Sterling receives the ball in the box, turns Joe Gomez and tries to escape his close attention before being brought down to give ref Anthony Taylor a simple decision to point to the spot. Kevin De Bruyne coolly sends Alisson the wrong way to put City 1-0 up.

26

9 November 2003

In the last Manchester derby at Maine Road, City fans demanded nothing less than a win against United. City had struck first through Nicolas Anelka but United levelled quickly through Ole Gunnar Solskjaer. It was nervy, frantic stuff but Maine Road was in raptures again on 26 minutes with a goal the Blues' fans might have scripted themselves. Gary Neville's attempt to shepherd a ball out of play for a goal kick is foiled by Shaun Goater who nicks the ball away from the Reds' defender to leave the Bermudian with just keeper Fabien Barthez to beat – and his crisp low shot does exactly that to put City 2-1 up. It was a nightmare moment for Neville who was left wishing the ground would open and swallow him but for Goater, it was the start of a magical afternoon as he moved on to 99 goals for the Blues against the side he once played for.

21 February 2017

City strike first in a Champions League round of 16 first leg against Monaco at the Etihad. In what will prove an eight-goal classic, David Silva threads a pass through to Leroy Sane who takes the ball in his stride before crossing low into the six-yard box for Raheem Sterling to sweep home from close range and put the Blues 1-0 up.

5 April 2017

Trailing 1-0 to Premier League leaders Chelsea, City playmaker David Silva sees his shot well saved by Thibaut Courtois at the near post, but the Belgian keeper can only push the ball out to the edge of the six-yard box where Sergio Aguero is waiting to pounce quicker than anyone else to level the scores at Stamford Bridge against the champions-elect.

18 May 2019

David Silva puts City ahead as the Blues go looking for a fourth domestic trophy of the campaign. Having already secured the Premier League, Carabao Cup and Community Shield, City are aiming to become the first side to achieve a domestic clean sweep, and the demolition of Watford in the FA Cup Final begins when Raheem Sterling heads a clearance back into the box and Silva holds off a challenge to send an angled shot past the keeper and put City 1-0 up at Wembley against Watford.

27

19 May 1999

One of the most important goals City legend Shaun Goater ever scores seals a place at Wembley for the Blues. Having drawn the Division Two play-off semi-final first leg with Wigan Athletic 1-1, the second leg at Maine Road was always going to be tense – but the game is settled by a controversial Goater goal as Michael Brown whips in a cross from the right and the Bermudian striker bundles the ball home from somewhere just above his left hip – Wigan protest it was handball (and still do to this day), but the goal stands and City hold on to win 1-0 and go to the play-off final as a result.

29 December 2001

City double their advantage over second-tier leaders Burnley, previously unbeaten in ten matches. The second goal comes after 27 minutes when Ali Benarbia plays in Paulo Wanchope who finishes coolly for his second of the afternoon.

14 April 2012

An absolute beauty of a goal puts City 2-0 up at Carrow Road. Sergio Aguero heads towards the Norwich box and plays a short pass to Carlos Tevez who back-heels the ball back into Sergio's path and the striker thunders an unstoppable shot from 18 yards out, high into the top left-hand corner of the net to give keeper John Ruddy no chance and double the Blues' lead.

22 April 2014

Relegation-threatened Wolves resist for as long as they can but finally, City break the deadlock. Gael Clichy's excellent ball puts Sergio Aguero clear in the box and though he begins to stumble as the keeper rushes out, Kun still has the nous to poke the ball past him and into the net from close range to give title-chasing City a crucial lead.

20 August 2016

City take the lead away to Stoke. As a corner comes in, Potters defender Ryan Shawcross tugs Nicolas Otamendi's shirt and the infringement is spotted by the referee, who duly awards a penalty. Sergio Aguero, despite missing two spot kicks four days earlier against Steaua Bucharest in the Champions League qualifier second leg, makes no mistake with a powerful right-foot drive to the keeper's left to put the Blues 1-0 up.

16 September 2017

The first of yet another hat-trick for Sergio Aguero against Watford – and his second career treble against the Hornets. Kevin De Bruyne's superb free kick into the box is begging to be headed by someone and – of course – Aguero obliges, being the first to arrive and plants a firm header to Heurelho Gomes's right to make it 1-0 at Vicarage Road.

28

15 October 2011

Mario Balotelli had quickly become the bane of Aston Villa due to a league hat-trick at Christmas 2010 and a superb goal in City's FA Cup victory in March 2011. But there was more to come ... Chasing an ambitious pass from Nigel de Jong, Balotelli reaches the ball before former City skipper Richard Dunne, but is unable to get the ball under control as his momentum takes him off the pitch, sliding in front of the advertising hoardings. A loud cheer from the away fans follows, which Mario responds to by staring at them with his finger to his lips in a shushing suggestion. When a corner on the half-hour mark hits Micah Richards and bounces in front of Balotelli, the striker improvises with a stunning overhead finish, giving City their first goal of the day. Pushing his onrushing team-mates aside, Mario returns to the area in front of the Villa supporters, and delivers a telling glare in their direction.

27 April 2013

City have long accepted the title would not be coming back to the Etihad for a second successive season but still want to finish the campaign on a high. West Ham United defend well in the opening stages but Samir Nasri's dart to the byline and low cross gives Sergio

Aguero a clear sight of goal and he makes no mistake with a left-foot shot from six yards out.

10 December 2013

After falling 2-0 behind to Pep Guardiola's Bayern Munich in the opening 12 minutes, it looked to be only a matter of how many Bayern Munich would score against City at the Allianz Arena. But City dig in and start what will be a remarkable comeback when Jesus Navas's cross is headed back across goal by James Milner and David Silva prods home from close range to halve the deficit in the final Group D Champions League clash.

13 September 2014

Another Sergio Aguero goal created by Jesus Navas. The Spain winger manages to keep the ball in on the right flank before carrying play to the corner of the Arsenal box, picking out Aguero's clever run and delivering a low cross that the Argentine turns in from the edge of the six-yard box to put City 1-0 up at the Emirates.

14 September 2016

Another penalty clinically dispatched by Sergio Aguero after Ilkay Gundogan is fouled inside the box. It puts City 2-0 up against German side Borussia Monchengladbach in a group-stage Champions League clash at the Etihad Stadium.

29 October 2016

When he's at his best, Sergio Aguero is simply unstoppable – as this howitzer of a goal proves, the brilliant Argentinian is at the peak of his powers. After almost wrestling the ball off David Silva, Aguero strikes a beautiful curling shot into the top-right corner for his second of the game and to give City a 2-0 lead away to West Brom.

12 May 2019

Having just gone behind to a Glenn Murray header in a game City had to win to seal the 2018/19 Premier League title, it takes City just 83 seconds to level the scores against Brighton & Hove Albion at the Amex Stadium. As a ball is played towards David Silva, he manages the slightest of back-flicks into the path of Sergio Aguero who hits a low drive through the keeper's legs to make it 1-1.

29

7 November 1987

City double the lead against Huddersfield Town at Maine Road. Neil McNab finds Tony Adcock on the edge of the Terriers' box and his clever prod frees Paul Stewart in the box – he collects the pass and nudges the ball forward before drilling a low shot across the keeper and into the bottom-left corner to make it 2-0.

21 December 2011

The scrappiest goal of Sergio Aguero's career so far – but nobody at the Etihad is complaining. Yaya Toure hits a low shot that Vincent Kompany turns goalwards, but Stoke City keeper Thomas Sorensen parries the shot across goal to the lurking Aguero who has the simplest of tasks to tap into the empty net to put City ahead.

21 October 2014

City grab a vital Champions League goal away to CSKA. In freezing conditions in Moscow, Edin Dzeko powers into the Russians' box and, with only the keeper to beat, unselfishly passes to his right where Sergio Aguero has the simple task of planting the ball into the empty net and put the Blues 1-0 up.

3 May 2015

A beauty at White Hart Lane! A typical defence-splitting pass from David Silva allows Sergio Aguero to surge into the Tottenham box and the Argentine striker takes a quick glance before hitting an angled shot over Hugo Lloris to score what proves to be the only goal of the game.

17 October 2015

Having already scored on seven minutes, a confident Raheem Sterling picks the ball up on the left and darts towards the Bournemouth box, cutting inside, before feigning a shot. As one defender goes to ground, another one shapes up to block any goal-bound effort and again, Sterling feigns a shot and the defender takes the bait. It all happens in a split second and Sterling, now with a clear view of the goal, tucks the ball home from eight yards for a quite stunning solo effort as City go 3-0 up against the Cherries at the Etihad.

30

9 May 1981

Tommy Hutchison was a genius and a delight to watch. Part of the fabled Tartan Trio that included Bobby McDonald and Gerry Gow who helped transform a sorry City team into a slick, solid side that specialised in cup ties, he was sadly at the wrong end of what should have been a glittering career. His silky skills, vision and trickery made him an instant favourite with the City fans and it was perhaps fitting that he should score City's opening goal of the 1981 FA Cup Final. As the Blues pressed for an opener, the ball found its way to Ray Ranson on the right flank and he whips in a perfect ball that Hutchison launches himself at, connects sweetly and heads home to put his side 1-0 up. A goal worthy of winning a cup final, though Hutch will famously score a late own goal, resulting in a replay five days later.

10 May 2011

It was strange that the matter of Champions League qualification should be fought between the same two teams in the exact same fixture at the end of two consecutive seasons. Even stranger then that the decisive goal should be scored by the exact same player! Having missed out to a solitary Peter Crouch goal the season before, City were desperate to qualify for the Champions League at the second time of asking. Poetic justice, then, that England international Crouch would again score the decisive goal – this time past his own goalkeeper! Crouch turns in James Milner's cross to give the Blues a 1-0 lead and – finally – entry into Europe's elite competition.

1 March 2017

Leroy Sane finally pulls City level against Championship promotion-chasers Huddersfield Town in an FA Cup fifth-round replay at the Etihad. Former City Academy striker Harry Bunn had stunned the home fans with an early strike, but despite holding out until a third of the way through the game, Raheem Sterling's low cross means a simple tap-in for Sane makes it 1-1.

21 October 2017

An historic goal in its own right as, finally, Sergio Aguero draws level with City's record goalscorer Eric Brook as he plants home his 177th goal for the Blues from the spot. There's a whiff of controversy as Burnley argue with the referee's decision to award a penalty following Bernardo Silva's clash with Clarets keeper Nick Pope. Sergio ignores the fuss and focuses on the job in hand before calmly sending Pope the wrong way to officially write his name into the Manchester City history books as the Blues' all-time joint-top goalscorer. Now, time to set a new record ...

1 March 2020

City's grip on the Carabao Cup tightens as the Blues go 2-0 up against Aston Villa. Leading from a Sergio Aguero goal ten minutes before, the second of the final at Wembley is a set piece, as Ilkay Gundogan's whipped-in corner is powerfully headed home by Rodrigo to put Pep Guardiola's side in command and on the way to a third successive Carabao Cup triumph.

31

19 August 2007

Geovanni arrived at City as something of an unknown quantity, but a debut goal against West Ham United on the opening weekend had made him an instant hit with the Blues' fans who quickly took to his creative, energetic style of play. A midweek home debut against Aston Villa had seen the Brazilian again impress and the Blues took their 100% record into the third game of the campaign – a Manchester derby against United. With an electrically charged atmosphere inside the Etihad Stadium, City take the game to the Reds on a warm, summer afternoon. What will prove to be the only goal of the match comes when Geovanni picks up the ball fully 30 yards out and cracks a low shot with the outside of his right foot that swerves out and then in as it flies past Edwin van der Sar on 31 minutes.

24 July 2011

Mario Balotelli had already given City the lead from the penalty spot during a pre-season friendly versus LA Galaxy at the Home Depot Arena, but the Italian striker makes the headlines for a different reason entirely on this occasion. Presented with a goalscoring opportunity after a defence-splitting pass from David Silva, Balotelli attempts an intricate back-heel pirouette to place the ball past the goalkeeper. Unfortunately, he misses the goal. Roberto Mancini is far from impressed and immediately substitutes his Italian protégé who protests with the manager, claiming that he thought he was offside before attempting the fanciful effort – with his body language perhaps backing up the striker's story. An eventful end to the America tour regardless and a lesson learned, perhaps.

16 August 2015

What a start to the new campaign for City and Sergio Aguero as the Blues thrash Chelsea 3-0 at the Etihad. Yaya Toure plays a simple pass into Aguero who chests the ball down, shows fantastic close control to edge it away from a defender to open up a yard of space and then calmly rolls a shot past Chelsea keeper Asmir Begovic to put City 1-0 up.

16 September 2017

A second in four minutes for Sergio Aguero makes it 2-0 as David Silva's clever early pass catches the Watford defence cold and it's an easy tap-in for Kun at the far post on what will be a long afternoon for the Hornets.

32

1 April 1991

Niall Quinn bags the first of what will be his first Manchester City hat-trick away to Crystal Palace. City attack down the right with David White feeding Ged Brannan and his cross is turned in at the far post with Quinn's left foot to make it 1-0.

16 March 1996

It was one of those moments when you just had to be there. On paper, it didn't look like the most appetising game with relegation-threatened City hosting fellow strugglers Southampton. The Blues, desperate for a win, had clawed their way back from the dead after a dreadful start but just two wins from 14 left Alan Ball's side in peril of dropping out of the Premier League for the first time since its 1992 inception. Giorgi Kinkladze had been the Blues' shining light during the start of what would be a dark period for the club, but his grace and skill were perhaps suited to a more prestigious stage than a relegation battle. On a damp, grey Manchester afternoon, however, the little Georgian would leave the Maine Road crowd breathless with possibly the greatest goal the old stadium had ever witnessed. Kinky picks the ball up on the right flank before suddenly accelerating past his marker who chases in vain, hacking at the Georgian without connecting. There are still four defenders ahead of him on the edge of the box, but he drops a shoulder, glides past two of the challenges with ridiculous ease and then is faced with Southampton keeper Dave Beasant – but instead of rushing his shot he waits, feigns and then gently lifts the ball over the stranded keeper to put City ahead. It was a moment of pure genius and a superb individual effort from a very gifted footballer.

22 September 2001

Having fallen behind to Sheffield Wednesday with just three minutes on the clock, City draw level at Hillsborough. Stuart Pearce's corner is half-cleared to Ali Benarbia, who drops his shoulder, cuts inside and hits a low shot from the left corner of the Owls box and squeezes the ball between keeper Kevin Pressman and his right-hand post to make it 1-1.

3 December 2011

This was a goal that almost had to be seen to be believed. Micah Richards's burst into the box sees the right-back squeeze a cross into the feet of Aguero. With five players surrounding him he drops his shoulder to go one way, putting two defenders off balance before toe-poking the ball home from six yards through a proverbial forest of legs to give the Blues a 1-0 lead against Norwich City at the Etihad.

8 November 2014

A classic goal from one of the world's best strikers levels the scores at Loftus Road. There's something about playing QPR that brings out the best in Sergio Aguero and this game is a case in point. Aguero chases a long pass from Eliaquim Mangala before expertly bringing the ball down, volleying it up gently before dropping his shoulder to the left and planting the ball past the keeper for a quite sublime goal.

33

1 April 1991

Two in two minutes for Niall Quinn who doubles City's lead against Crystal Palace with a stunning volley. David White races down the right flank before spotting Quinn's dart towards the box – he flights the perfect cross to Quinn who volleys a sweet drive into the top-right corner from 12 yards to give Nigel Martyn no chance and put the Blues 2-0 up at Selhurst Park.

27 November 2013

Sergio Aguero is fouled as he crosses the ball into the Plzen box and a penalty is awarded by the referee. Aguero dusts himself down to take the penalty and he makes no mistake from the spot as he sends the keeper the wrong way with a low shot to the left to put City 1-0 up in the Champions League group-stage clash at the Etihad.

2 February 2015

A battling goal and one made and scored by Sergio Aguero at his very best. After winning a tussle just inside the Stoke City half, Aguero bursts forward, weighs up his options, before going inside the box and firing a low right-foot shot into the bottom left-hand corner of the net to give City a 1-0 lead at the Britannia Stadium.

7 January 2020

City double their lead at Old Trafford in the Carabao Cup semi-final first leg. The Blues had been knocking at the door continually after going ahead through Bernardo, and it is the Portuguese who is again integral in the second. His slide-rule pass from the halfway line is perfectly weighted for Riyad Mahrez, who receives a helping hand from the outstretched leg of Victor Lindelof and with David De Gea caught in no man's land, the Algerian rounds him with ease to make it 2-0.

34

7 November 1987

City go 3-0 up against Huddersfield Town at Maine Road with a well-worked goal. Paul Lake brings the ball forward before playing a pass to the overlapping Andy Hinchcliffe on the left – the full-back manages to whip a ball into the centre where Tony Adcock arrives to thump a header past the keeper from point-blank range for his first league goal for the club.

28 August 2011

Edin Dzeko gets his first on what will be an unforgettable day for the Bosnian striker at White Hart Lane. Spurs had held out for the opening half hour, but the Blues were dangerous and it looked more a matter of 'when' rather than 'if' City would finally break through. Samir Nasri, making his City debut after joining from Spurs' arch-rivals Arsenal, set Dzeko on his way with a clever chip to the far post where Dzeko volleys home to make it 1-0 for the visitors.

23 October 2013

The first of another brace for Sergio Aguero comes in a Champions League group-stage clash against CSKA Moscow. David Silva races into the box on the left before picking out Aguero's clever run – he just nips in ahead of the defender and then slots it to the goalkeeper's left to put City level just two minutes after falling behind to the Russians.

23 November 2013

City go 2-0 up against Spurs with Hugo Lloris – badly at fault for the opening goal – again to blame for another poor clearance. City pick up the French keeper's kick and the ball goes out to Samir Nasri who crosses in from the left to Sergio Aguero who sees his shot saved, but Alvaro Negredo follows up with a shot that is blocked by Sandro who then bundles the ball into the back of the net with his other leg for an own goal.

2 July 2020

City continue to find space behind the Liverpool midfield and, on 34 minutes, it leads to a second goal as Phil Foden, Kevin De Bruyne and Raheem Sterling pour forward; De Bruyne acts as the decoy as Foden finds Sterling who takes one touch before rolling the ball past Alisson from close range to make it 2-0 to the Blues.

35

5 September 1981

City's record new £1m signing Trevor Francis marks his debut with a superb goal. Playing Stoke City at the Victoria Ground, more than 10,000 City fans had travelled to Staffordshire to watch the England forward's first game, and they were not disappointed. City dominate and Stoke hold out until the 35th minute when Bobby McDonald's long clearance finds new boy Francis running free in a promising position. He proceeds to turn the gangly Brendan O'Callaghan inside out before moving inside Ray Evans and again meeting O'Callaghan tracking back as best he can. Rounding the defender for a second time, Francis hits a low shot through Fox's legs to the delight of the Blues fans behind the goal and to give his new club a 1-0 lead. Francis will later add a second in the 3-1 win over the Potters.

23 September 1989

A rampant City go 3-0 up against Manchester United in a demolition derby at Maine Road. On a day when everything seemed to go right for Mel Machin's men, Steve Redmond wins possession just outside his own box and exchanges passes with David White. Redmond then sends a measured ball down the right flank for

David Oldfield who gets to the pass ahead of a defender and then sends the perfect cross into the middle where Ian Bishop arrives on cue to power a diving header past Jim Leighton and put City fans in dreamland.

22 September 2001

City go 2-1 up away to Sheffield Wednesday. Stuart Pearce's free kick causes confusion in the Owls box and, as Westwood attempts to shepherd the ball back to his keeper, Shaun Goater nips in to lob over keeper Kevin Pressman to score the Blues' second goal in three minutes at Hillsborough.

29 December 2001

City go 3-0 up in the second-tier clash with leaders Burnley at Maine Road. A slick interchange between Paulo Wanchope and Shaun Goater ends with Eyal Berkovic scoring from the edge of the box with a superb drive to leave the Clarets shell-shocked.

1 March 2017

Sergio Aguero sends a penalty powerfully past the Huddersfield Town goalkeeper after Nicolas Otamendi had been fouled in the box. It puts City 2-1 up against the Terriers who had earlier taken a shock lead at the Etihad.

36

19 April 2015

Great work from Jesus Navas sees the pacey Spanish winger burst down the right flank and into the West Ham United penalty area before delivering a pinpoint cross into the middle for Sergio Aguero to sweep home with ease and put City 2-0 up at the Etihad.

20 August 2016

City cruise into a 2-0 lead at the Britannia Stadium with yet another set piece resulting in a goal. Kevin De Bruyne whips a superb cross into the Stoke City box and finds the head of Sergio Aguero who expertly glances past the keeper from six yards out for his second of the afternoon.

10 September 2016

Kelechi Iheanacho deservedly puts City 2-0 up against Manchester United at Old Trafford. Kevin De Bruyne – scorer of the opening goal – sees a low shot strike the foot of the post and fall kindly to Iheanacho who makes no mistake from close range to put City firmly in command of the Manchester derby.

21 May 2017

Leroy Sane's dash past a static Watford defence to the byline sees the German winger pull the ball back into the path of Sergio Aguero, who sweeps the ball home from close range for his 33rd of the campaign – his best ever seasonal tally and proof that, if anything, he is getting better as he gets older! It also gives City a 3-0 lead at Vicarage Road.

37

26 November 2016

Not one for the purists but a vital goal all the same as City draw level with Burnley at Turf Moor. In what is one of Sergio Aguero's scrappiest goals for City, a scramble in the six-yard box from a corner sees Nicolas Otamendi divert the ball into Kun's path, and he stabs the ball home from two yards out.

9 September 2017

A major turning point in the game between City and Liverpool comes as Sadio Mane races through on to a lofted pass from Joel Matip and, as the Liverpool forward approaches the ball, Ederson bravely heads clear before crashing to the floor courtesy of Mane's high boot. Referee Jon Moss takes a moment – perhaps seeing the nasty gash on Ederson's head – before issuing a straight red for the Liverpool man for reckless play.

38

6 April 2016

City trailed 1-0 to Paris Saint-Germain after Fernando's dreadful error saw Zlatan Ibrahimovic – who had already missed a penalty – block the Brazilian's pass and the ball flew past Joe Hart for a bizarre opening goal for the French champions. Few of the so-called experts had given City much of a chance of coming away from the Parc des Princes with anything but a defeat, but the Blues hit back before the break in an enthralling Champions League quarter-final first leg. Fernandinho moves forward towards the PSG box before playing a pass to his right where Kevin De Bruyne takes a touch and then lashes a low shot past the keeper to make it 1-1.

1 March 2017

A rare goal for Pablo Zabaleta puts City 3-1 up and means the Blues have now scored three goals in just eight first-half minutes. It is a goal made in Argentina after Zabaleta thumps a shot into the top right-hand corner from close range after a cross from compatriot Sergio Aguero as the FA Cup fifth-round replay with Huddersfield Town starts to take a more predictable path.

12 May 2019

City take a 2-1 lead over Brighton in the final game of the 2018/19 campaign. Needing a win to seal the Premier League title, the Blues go ahead when Riyad Mahrez's deep corner finds the head of Aymeric Laporte who powers a header past Mat Ryan to put the destiny of the title back in City's hands.

18 May 2019

City go 2-0 up against Watford in the FA Cup Final at Wembley. Bernardo Silva clips a measured cross towards the back post where Gabriel Jesus manages to squeeze an angled shot that beats the keeper and just crosses the line before Raheem Sterling makes sure to put the Blues firmly in command.

7 January 2020

Bernardo's precision passing leads to a third City goal against Manchester United in the Carabao Cup semi-final first leg at Old Trafford. Bernardo releases Riyad Mahrez, who is initially thwarted by Brandon Williams's recovery tackle, but the youngster succeeds only in guiding the ball into Kevin De Bruyne's path. The Belgian leaves Phil Jones floundering with a drop of his shoulder, before drilling the ball at David De Gea and watching it rebound on to Andreas Pereira's leg and into the empty net to make it 3-0 on the night.

39

13 April 2002

It might not be the most memorable goal that the Blues have ever scored against Gillingham but Shaun Goater's strike towards the end of the 2001/02 season is just a little bit special. With the Division One title already wrapped up, Kevin Keegan's side play with the freedom of a club looking forward to the challenge of Premier League football and it shows. With the score 1-1 at the Priestfield Stadium, Goater plays a one-two with Algerian ace Ali Benarbia with the Goat meeting his team-mate's exquisite return flick with a superb volley that nestles in the bottom corner to put City 2-1 up.

13 May 2012

City finally take the lead in the 2011/12 Premier League title decider at the Etihad. With QPR defending for their lives, finally, Yaya Toure flicks the ball into the feet of Pablo Zabaleta who hits an angled shot towards goal where keeper Paddy Kenny can only push the ball up over his head before it dips in off the far post to make it 1-0 and sends the Etihad Stadium into raptures.

11 May 2014

On the final day of the campaign, the scenario for City was simple – a draw against West Ham would be enough to secure the Premier League title for the second time in three seasons with Liverpool's goal difference substantially inferior to that of City's no matter whether they beat Newcastle United at Anfield or not. West Ham had talked up the final game against the Blues, saying how they would make life difficult for the champions-elect – especially Liverpool fan Kevin Nolan – but City knew patience was the key. There was no need for anything rash, but by the same token, nobody wanted a scenario where it was late in the game with the scores still level, just in case. Yet as half-time approached, the Hammers were still holding firm. Then Samir Nasri picks the ball up in the Hammers' half, plays a short pass to Yaya Toure and then moves into space. Yaya plays him the ball back and Nasri, invited to push the ball forward by a tentative West Ham defence, suddenly unleashes a low shot from 20 yards that strikes the foot of the post on its way into the net. The celebrations began and from that point, the Blues were never going to throw away the advantage.

1 November 2016

City equalise against Barcelona in a Champions League group-stage clash at the Etihad. The goal comes as a result of a stray pass at the back by the Catalans that Sergio Aguero collects, plays it to the right where Raheem Sterling takes it on, crosses low into the middle and Ilkay Gundogan sweeps home with a powerful left-foot shot to make it 1-1.

40

4 May 1968

Knowing maximum points from the final two games of the 1967/68 season would mean City were top division champions for the first time since 1937 meant there was incredible pressure on the Blues to win away to a very good Spurs team looking to secure a finish that would at least make them London's top club – and then again at Newcastle United a week later. Manchester United were waiting for City to slip up and, if Joe Mercer's men did and the Reds won their remaining two games, the title would go to Old Trafford and not Maine Road. But City were in no mood to hand their opportunity away and despite both teams having good chances to score in the first half, the imperious Colin Bell finally breaks the deadlock just before half-time to send the travelling fans wild. It was the perfect time to score and was enough to take the visitors into the break 1-0 up.

3 August 1968

City score a third goal before the break to all but ensure victory in the 1968 Charity Shield clash with West Brom – and it's a goal that underlines just how brilliant and influential Colin Bell, Francis Lee and Mike Summerbee are to this magnificent Mercer/Allison side. A free kick on the edge of the box suggests Lee is shaping up to smash the ball goalwards – the crowd thought as much and the Albion defenders certainly are convinced, but Lee runs past the ball as Bell instead passes to Summerbee on the penalty spot: Buzzer then passes to the advancing Lee who has continued his run and the Blues' No.9 slots the ball home to make it 3-0. It is so simple, yet brilliant and innovative.

28 April 2000

How 12 months can turn a footballer's life upside down. In May 1999, Robert Taylor had been one of the scorers as Gillingham opened up a 2-0 lead in the 1999 Division Two play-off final at Wembley and with almost 90 minutes played in that game, the Gills simply couldn't miss out on promotion. Of course, they did, and Gillingham remained a third-tier side, but City came back to buy Robert Taylor and he repaid his transfer fee in full as he scores the only goal of the game against Birmingham City to leave the Blues needing just a point from the final game of the 1999/2000 season to win promotion back to the Premier League.

14 May 2013

City's first game following the dismissal of manager Roberto Mancini is away to Reading – but Sergio Aguero continues his fine run in sky blue with the opening goal of the game on 40 minutes. The result of a delightful triangular passing move, David Silva and James Milner combine with the latter's low cross turned in by Aguero with a smart right-foot finish from close range – his 17th and final goal of his second season at the club.

3 January 2019

City know that defeat to Liverpool in the Premier League would leave the Reds ten points clear at the halfway point of the 2018/19 campaign. It's a game City can't lose and the first goal was always going to be critical – and fortunately, it's City who get it. The superb Bernardo Silva slips a pass to Sergio Aguero on the corner of the six-yard box and after taking a touch, fires a powerful angled shot into the roof of the net to give Alisson no chance and put the defending champions 1-0 up.

41

7 November 1987

David White puts City 4-0 up against Huddersfield Town before the break as the Blues again punish the visitors' slack defending. Paul Simpson attacks down the left, but his low cross hits a defender and comes back to him. Undeterred, Simpson sizes up his options, drops his shoulder and takes out perhaps six static defenders as he gets to the byline, crossing into the middle where an unmarked David White has the simplest of tasks to guide a side-foot shot past the keeper.

28 August 2011

Edin Dzeko scores his second of the afternoon to double City's lead at White Hart Lane – and just as had been the case for the opener, it was Samir Nasri who provided the cross, finding Dzeko who expertly guides a header into the top-right corner to make it 2-0 in the North London sunshine.

19 November 2011

There can be no protestations when Newcastle United left-back Ryan Taylor clearly blocks Yaya Toure's goal-bound effort from close range with a raised arm. Toon goalkeeper Tim Krul does his best to put off City's new designated penalty taker Mario Balotelli by slyly kicking the ball from the penalty spot in an act that goes unpunished by referee Chris Foy and seemingly unnoticed by the TV cameras. It takes more than goalkeeper mind games to break the focus of Balotelli who, with an icy cool expression, nonchalantly runs up gently and strokes the ball home with consummate ease. What happened next was straight from the school of Balotelli as he celebrates by folding his arms and slowly walking towards the exacerbated Dutch goalkeeper. Only Mario!

23 November 2013

City go 3-0 up against Spurs at the Etihad. Jesus Navas receives the ball on the right flank and then delivers a low cross into the box for Sergio Aguero to cleverly guide into the bottom left-hand corner of Hugo Lloris's net.

16 January 2016

Slightly fortuitous by Sergio Aguero's standards, the City striker hits a shot from 25 yards that deflects off Crystal Palace defender Scott Dann's head and past the keeper to put City 2-0 up at the Etihad.

16 August 2016

Having missed two first-half penalties already, a determined Sergio Aguero soon makes opponents Steaua Bucharest pay with what will be the first goal of yet another hat-trick for the irrepressible Argentine. A ball on the edge of the Steaua box is controlled by

Raheem Sterling and Aguero does the rest, placing a shot past the home keeper in this Champions League play-off first leg.

42

19 January 2010

There's more than a whiff of controversy as City are awarded a penalty in the first leg of the League Cup semi-final against Manchester United at the Etihad. Trailing 1-0 to Ryan Giggs's early goal, Craig Bellamy skips down the left wing and towards the United box but, as he goes past Raphael da Silva, the Brazilian defender pulls him down; TV replays suggest the first foul was outside the box, but referee Mike Dean makes it clear it was for the second flailing arm that unbalanced the Welsh forward – and that was in the box – and so awards a penalty. Carlos Tevez thumps home the spot kick before running off to celebrate in front of the United fans and then wind up Gary Neville as City draw level at 1-1.

23 October 2013

Alvaro Negredo digs out a clever cross just inside the CSKA Moscow box and Sergio Aguero bravely arrives just before the goalkeeper to head home from close range and put City on the way to a vital 2-1 away win in Russia during a Champions League group-stage clash.

3 October 2015

City trail 1-0 to Newcastle until David Silva's clever chip finds Fernandinho, who heads across the six-yard box, and Sergio Aguero is well placed to head home the equaliser from close range. It's the first goal of what will be an incredible afternoon for the Argentine striker.

5 March 2017

Another assist for Raheem Sterling as his evolving understanding of Sergio Aguero's movements brings yet more reward. Sterling's clever low pass into the six-yard box allows Aguero to nip in between two defenders before dinking the ball past the keeper to give City a 1-0 lead away to Sunderland.

2 April 2017

Having just watched Arsenal score at the other end to make it 1-1, the Blues regain the lead with the tried and trusted partnership of David Silva and Sergio as the Spaniard slips a ball into the box to Kun who, from a tight angle, buries a low shot past David Ospina to put City back in front with a 2-1 lead at the Emirates.

43

29 April 1970

Leading 1-0 in a rain-sodden Prater Stadium, City double their lead in the European Cup Winners' Cup Final against Polish side Gornik Zabrze. Neil Young wins the ball after loose play from Florenski and breaks free towards goal. As Young moves into the penalty area, goalkeeper Hubert Kostka rushes out of his goal and upends the City forward, leaving the referee no option but to give a penalty. Francis Lee strikes the spot kick with power into the centre of the goal and, though Kostka's legs make contact with the ball, the force of the shot carries it into the net to make it 2-0 – a goal that will be enough to secure a final victory of 2-1 and City's first major European trophy.

15 August 2007

To say goals at the Etihad had been in short supply was something of an understatement. City fans had endured an incredibly barren run under Stuart Pearce's tenure with no home goals since New Year's Day 2007 which equated to 227 days without a goal to celebrate at the Etihad – easily the worst in the club's history. Sven-Goran Eriksson had taken over during the summer and had begun life as the Blues' boss with a 2-0 win at West Ham United on the opening day of the 2007/08 season.

City were hosting Derby County and surely this bleak run would finally end? As half-time approaches, the Rams are still holding the Blues 0-0 when, finally, the deadlock is broken. After such a lengthy wait, it needed to be something special – and it was. Michael Johnson pushes the ball past one challenge just inside his own half and accelerates forward. He spots Elano and plays the ball into the Brazilian's feet to get past another player and Elano returns the pass into Johnson's path as he moves towards goal. There is still plenty to do as a challenge is about to come in but Johnson gets there first, fires a rising shot with the outside of his right foot to score a superbly crafted goal. It proves to be the only goal of the game and comes after exactly 13 hours of scoreless football.

29 September 2012

Sergio Aguero bags his first goal of the 2012/13 season as Carlos Tevez fires a shot in that is guided goalwards by David Silva, only for Fulham's Mark Schwarzer to make an amazing save – but Aguero is first to the loose ball and he has the easiest of tap-ins from two yards to get his season up and running almost two months into the campaign.

24 April 2016

Goal number 28 of another prolific campaign for Sergio Aguero who makes no mistake from the penalty spot to put the Blues 2-0 up against Stoke City after Kelechi Iheanacho is brought down by Ryan Shawcross in the penalty area. The penalty has extra edge as former team-mate Shay Given is in goal for Stoke who now trail 2-0 at the Etihad.

5 November 2016

Sergio Aguero scores his landmark 150th goal for City at home to Middlesbrough. The milestone strike comes from close range as Aguero turns in Kevin De Bruyne's superb cross from the right on an otherwise frustrating afternoon for the Blues, who will lead 1-0 until added time against Boro who snatch a 1-1 draw at the Etihad.

10 December 2017

David Silva puts City ahead in the Manchester derby at Old Trafford. A corner from the right causes confusion in the United box and the ball falls to Silva who hooks a shot past David De Gea from close range to give the Blues a 1-0 lead.

44

15 September 1976

Taking on the mighty Juventus in the UEFA Cup first round, first leg at Maine Road, City battled to break down the Italians' resolute rear-guard. It was crucial the Blues took a lead over to Turin for the second leg and Dennis Tueart, Brian Kidd, Peter Barnes and Joe Royle had caused the Serie A giants headaches throughout the opening period – and the forwards' collective reward came when, after 44 minutes, former Manchester United striker Kidd sent a firm header past Dino Zoff following Tueart's corner and Royle's flick-on. It would be enough to secure a 1-0 win for Tony Book's men, though it wouldn't be enough to progress with the Old Lady securing a 2-0 victory in the return.

29 December 2001

With City's irrepressible midfield duo of Ali Benarbia and Eyal Berkovic at their brilliant best, the Blues continue to dissect the defence of second-tier leaders Burnley at Maine Road with a fourth goal before the break. The Clarets were simply being outclassed while City were sending out a message that would send a shudder down the rest of the division's spine. The move ends with Berkovic again slipping the ball perfectly through to Paulo Wanchope and the Costa Rican, in a carbon copy of his second goal, calmly slots the ball past Michopoulos to make it 4-0 at the break and complete a first-half hat-trick in the process.

21 November 2016

City had been systematically taken apart by Jurgen Klopp's Liverpool and were 3-0 down with barely 30 minutes played. Taking the bull by the horns, Sergio Aguero picks the ball up on the left, bamboozles Lucas Leiva, before hitting a fierce right-foot shot past Simon Mignolet from fully 20 yards out to give City a glimmer of hope.

11 July 2020

City continue to dominate away to Brighton and Gabriel Jesus finally gets a reward for his industry and effort. Kevin De Bruyne's corner finds the head of Rodrigo and his downward angled header is turned home by Jesus from a yard out – his 20th of the campaign.

45

3 April 2010

Carlos Tevez – already with one goal and one assist – sends a delightful threaded pass to set Emmanuel Adebayor clear on goal and the City striker makes no mistake, coolly slotting past Brian Jensen to give the Blues an incredible 5-0 half-time lead away to a shell-shocked Burnley.

5 October 2013

A goal made by the vision of David Silva and finished by the excellence of Sergio Aguero. There seems to be little on as Silva drives forward towards the Everton box, then, as Aguero makes a clever dart to the right, Silva looks as though he will play it to his left before playing a pass into Kun's path and his first-time angled shot gives Toffees keeper Tim Howard no chance on his near post to make it 2-1 to City at the Etihad. Clinical.

2 July 2020

An intricate passing move on the edge of the Liverpool box sees Phil Foden flick the ball to Kevin De Bruyne and then spin into space for the return where the young midfielder fires over the diving Alisson and makes it 3-0 in the behind-closed-doors clash at the Etihad.

45+1

30 April 2012

In what was labelled as the biggest Manchester derby of all time, how fitting that the City skipper should decide the outcome. In essence, with three games to go and City and United locked in a battle for the title, this was the game that would almost certainly decide the destination of the Premier League crown. The Blues' superior goal difference meant a win would put them level on points with United and above them at the top of the table. A win for United would mean the Reds needed one more point from their remaining two matches to clinch the title. A draw would also suit United. City started like a team who knew it was now or never, taking the game to the Reds who sat back, looking as though they had come for a draw with the idea they might also nick a winner at some point. While United were cautious, the Blues threw caution to the wind and, as the board for first-half added time goes up, City win a corner on the left. David Silva whips the ball in and it is captain Vincent Kompany who rises higher than anyone else to powerfully head the ball past David De Gea for what will be the only goal of the game. It just had to be the captain, and the win puts the destiny of the title firmly in City's hands for the first time. It wasn't spectacular, but it meant everything ...

45+6

9 September 2017

City increase the lead over ten-man Liverpool at the Etihad. Gabriel Jesus – who had just seen a goal chalked off – meets Kevin De Bruyne's excellent cross from the left of the Liverpool box and plants a header firmly past Simon Mignolet to make it 2-0 over the Merseysiders.

Second half

46

4 May 1968

Having struck just before the break in the penultimate game of the 1967/68 campaign, Joe Mercer and Malcolm Allison knew Spurs would come back strongly after the break. With a crowd of more than 51,000 packed inside White Hart Lane, the dream scenario for the champions-elect was, of course, to kill the game off as quickly as possible, and within a minute of the restart Colin Bell bagged his second of the game and made it 2-0 to give the Blues vital breathing space. It was just as well because Spurs piled on the pressure from then on and City's efforts in the first half – and over an epic season – began to show in the form of fatigue. Had the hosts, who hit the woodwork twice, taken any of their numerous chances, it would have been a severe test of City's durability in the last third of the game.

28 February 1976

With the teams emerging from the dressing room at the break at 1-1, City and Newcastle United resume battle in the 1976 League Cup Final at Wembley. City race out of the blocks and, in the first minute of the second period, there seems little danger for Newcastle United as City full-back Willie Donachie whips in a cross from the left. The ball is met by Tommy Booth's header, at the back of the six-yard box, and as the ball loops into the heart of the Newcastle penalty area, Dennis Tueart launches a perfectly timed and executed overhead kick. The ball powers past helpless Newcastle keeper Mike Mahoney into the right-hand corner of the net for what will prove to be the goal that secures a 2-1 win for the Blues.

18 September 2011

Edin Dzeko leaps to head down a long ball forward into the path of Aguero. In a flash, the Argentina star takes one touch before firing a low shot from 20 yards out that arrows into the bottom corner past Schwarzer to double City's lead against Fulham.

47

14 April 2013

A first for Sergio Aguero in a City shirt – a headed goal – and one worthy of settling this FA Cup semi-final at Wembley. City, leading 1-0, start the second period in ideal fashion as Gareth Barry lofts a tempting cross into the Chelsea box for Aguero to leap highest and send a looping header past Petr Cech and all but secure the Blues' place in the FA Cup Final for the second time in three years.

22 September 2013

What better way to celebrate reaching the 50-goal mark than to start your next half-century? City increase the lead over Manchester United with a goal that highlights the Reds' defensive frailties as Sergio Aguero is again allowed too much space and time to score his second of the afternoon. The creator this time is Alvaro Negredo who is able to turn easily just inside the box. He whips in a cross that Aguero volleys with enough power to beat David De Gea for the second time in a little over half an hour as the rampant Blues open up a three-goal lead.

48

4 February 2004

Ten-man City, trailing 3-0 away to Tottenham in the FA Cup, pull a goal back just after the break to spark an incredible comeback. The excellent Michael Tarnat floats a ball towards the six-yard box where Spurs, perhaps a little too relaxed given the situation, allow a galloping Sylvain Distin enough space to fashion a header – of sorts – past Kasey Keller to make it 3-1 and give Kevin Keegan's side a glimmer of hope.

8 April 2017

Sometimes a goal can take your breath away. Whether it's a stunning volley from 30 yards, an individual mazy run and goal or some acrobatic effort that you'll see repeated a thousand times over – we all know a 'worldy' when we see it. Less common is a team goal. All too often we'll focus on the end product – how the ball is dispatched into the net – but if that were the case in this instance, this goal wouldn't have even made it into the Top 200. From start to finish, however, this goal was a thing of beauty. To list every player's contribution and what part they played would need an extra couple of pages, but all 11 City players were involved over the course of a minute or so. It all begins with a Gael Clichy throw-in on the left and then the passes begin and for all Hull's attempted pressing, they can't get anywhere near the ball. After spreading play around at the back, suddenly, the pace shifts up a couple of gears until Yaya Toure plays a fast pass into David Silva's feet, he finds Raheem Sterling who drifts past one challenge into the box, beats another defender and crosses it into the six-yard box where Sergio Aguero scuffs a shot that bobbles over the line. The goal was the worst part of the move, ironically, and Aguero half-nodded at the finish, almost in disappointment as the 23-pass sequence ended and the only Hull touch was the attempt to stop the ball on the goal line. As a result, City go 2-0 up.

49

29 October 2013

As good as any goal you're likely to see considering it was scored by Sergio Aguero's 'wrong' foot. City are trailing 1-0 to Chelsea at Stamford Bridge when Samir Nasri nudges the ball into Aguero's path and in a flash, the Argentina star rifles a left-foot shot high into the top left-hand corner of the net to level the scores – a fantastic goal.

11 May 2014

That man Vincent Kompany does it again – a big man for the big moments, the skipper effectively seals the Premier League title as he fires in from close range to put City 2-0 up against West Ham United. In what is a game City can afford to draw and still be crowned champions, Manuel Pellegrini's side do exactly what is needed, and when a corner hits the back of Edin Dzeko, Kompany turns home the loose ball to seal three points and a second title in three years for the Blues.

3 October 2015

Feeding off a pass from David Silva, Sergio Aguero works himself a yard of space on the edge of the Newcastle United box before firing a left-foot shot that deflects past Tim Krul to put City ahead. Untidy, but they all count!

28 February 2016

Fernandinho puts City 1-0 up in the 2016 Carabao Cup Final against Liverpool. Sergio Aguero collects a lofted pass from the left on the edge of the Liverpool box, controls and then waits for Fernandinho's overlapping run on the right – he slips a short ball into his path and the Brazilian hits a low shot that squirms under keeper Simon Mignolet to put the Blues ahead.

50

3 August 1968

West Brom's day gets worse as they go 4-1 down in the FA Charity Shield clash with City at Maine Road. The Baggies' sub goalkeeper's first job is to pick the ball out of the net after he allows Bobby Owen's tame shot to somehow emerge from under his dive and trickle over the line.

14 May 1981

City fans dare to dream as Kevin Reeves puts the Blues 2-1 up in the Centenary FA Cup Final at Wembley. As Dave Bennett drives into the Spurs box, he is sandwiched by a combination of Tottenham defenders Paul Miller and Chris Hughton and referee Keith Hackett points to the penalty spot. Reeves steps up and though the keeper guesses correctly, the ball is hit with pace into the bottom right-hand corner to put John Bond's side ahead.

11 January 2003

It's not often a left-back scores a worldy – unless they are Brazilian, so we are often told. In January 2003, one City left-back scored not only the goal of his life, but perhaps the last great goal scored at Maine Road. The Blues had made a more than respectable return to the Premier League under the leadership of Kevin Keegan and were comfortably placed in mid-table. Leeds United were on the wane having finished fifth the previous season and were a team in decline, but they had still dished out a 3-0 opening-day defeat to Keegan's side. The goal that proves to be the winner comes when Nicolas Anelka sizes up his options as the Blues attack, spots Niclas Jensen's run towards the box on the left and chips the ball into the Danish defender's path and without hesitation he immaculately volleys a shot that flies past Paul Robinson like a rocket, giving the Lilywhites' keeper no chance whatsoever.

9 November 2003

A dream moment for former Manchester United youth player Shaun Goater as he scores his 100th City goal in the last ever Manchester derby to be played at Maine Road. Phil Neville loses the ball in his own half and Niclas Jensen tees up Eyal Berkovic who immediately guides a superbly controlled pass between two United defenders and Goater does the rest, lifting the ball over Fabien Barthez to score his 100th City goal. Fairy-tale stuff.

29 December 2012

City start like a house on fire with Edin Dzeko scoring twice in the first four minutes, but when Samir Nasri is sent off later in the half and the hosts reduce the deficit, it looks like being a long afternoon for the Blues.

But Yaya Toure's vision sets free Aguero who holds off the challenge of Sebastien Bassong to lift the ball over the keeper and restore City's two-goal advantage over Norwich City at Carrow Road.

23 November 2013

Sergio Aguero bags his second of the afternoon and City's fourth as the Blues continue to dissect Spurs at the Etihad. The goal is all the work of Yaya Toure, who picks up possession deep in his own half before playing one neat one-two to get around a challenge, then another on the halfway line before powerfully bursting towards the Tottenham box and passing to his right where the unmarked Aguero calmly slots a first-time shot past Hugo Lloris to make it 4-0. Brilliant from Yaya.

10 May 2015

Sergio Aguero's second goal of the game comes as a QPR defender attempts to control a clearance on the halfway line but instead gives the ball to Aguero, who sprints towards goal before coolly slotting the ball past the keeper from ten yards to make it 3-0 – though he hadn't finished punishing the Hoops quite yet ...

3 October 2015

A moment of club history. Great vision from Kevin De Bruyne releases Sergio Aguero who runs in behind the Newcastle United defence, waiting for the goalkeeper to come towards him before he gently lifts the ball over

Tim Krul and into the far corner of the net – a third goal in eight minutes and City's quickest hat-trick ever. But Kun's day was far from over ...

5 March 2016

Former City defender Micah Richards is a shade unfortunate as he attempts to clear a ball into the Aston Villa box, only to see his tackle cannon off the shins of ex-team-mate Sergio Aguero and into the net as City go 2-0 up with a second goal in three minutes at the Etihad.

6 January 2017

Already 3-0 up in the FA Cup third-round tie away to West Ham United, City all but seal a place in the next round with goal number four. Raheem Sterling darts into the box on the left, checks back, spots Yaya Toure on the edge of the box and his shot is flicked home via the post by Sergio on the edge of the six-yard box for his first goal at the London Stadium – and the Blues' fourth of the game.

Dennis Tueart's spectacular overhead kick wins the 1976 League Cup Final against Newcastle United.

City's greatest ever goal – Sergio Aguero scores the winner against QPR in 2012 with the clock time at 93 minutes and 20 seconds.

'No Vinnie, No!' The words of thousands before Vincent Kompany hits a spectacular winner against Leicester City in May 2019 to put City one win away from another Premier League title.

Centurions! Gabriel Jesus scores the 94th-minute winner against Southampton on the final day of the 2017/18 season to bring up 100 points.

Richard Edghill emphatically strikes home his spot-kick in the 1999 play-off final penalty shoot-out against Gillingham.

Sergio Aguero salutes the City fans after becoming the club's all-time leading goalscorer. His goal away to Napoli in November 2017 took him to 178 for the Blues.

What a way to score your 100th goal for City as Shaun Goater puts the Blues 3-1 up against Manchester United in the last Maine Road derby in 2002.

Andy Hinchcliffe celebrates putting City 5-1 up against Manchester United in the September 1989 derby.

Tommy Hutchison celebrates putting City ahead in the 1981 FA Cup Final against Tottenham along with fellow Scots Bobby McDonald (left) and Gerry Gow (right).

Francis Lee celebrates at the Gallowgate End after putting City 4-2 up against Newcastle United – effectively the goal that sealed a first top flight title for 31 years.

Unbridled joy for Samir Nasri after he had powered home a superb goal against Sunderland in the 2014 Capital One Cup Final at Wembley.

Yaya Toure ends City's 35-year wait for a major trophy as he powers home the winning goal of the 2011 FA Cup Final against Stoke.

Legend – David Silva puts City 1-0 up against Watford in the 2019 FA Cup Final at Wembley.

Colin Bell levels for City against Spurs in the famous 'Ballet on Ice' clash in December 1967 at Maine Road.

Kevin De Bruyne celebrates after smashing a superb shot in off the underside of the crossbar to put City ahead against Newcastle United at St James' Park in November 2019.

51

19 October 2013

Sergio Aguero scores his second of the game to give City a 2-0 lead against West Ham United at Upton Park. The goal comes six minutes into the second half as the Argentine heads home David Silva's free kick from the right with ease thanks to some woeful marking by the home defence.

1 November 2016

Kevin De Bruyne gives City a 2-1 lead over Barcelona with a stunning free kick. The Blues had trailed to a Lionel Messi goal before Ilkay Gundogan levelled, but when a foul is awarded 20 yards from the Barca goal and slightly to the left, De Bruyne places the ball down before sending a dipping, powerful shot over the wall and into the top-right of the net to put Pep Guardiola's side ahead for the first time.

52

7 November 1987

City continue where they'd left off in the first half to go 5-0 up against Huddersfield Town. Paul Stewart collects a ball out of defence on the halfway line and finds Paul Simpson on the left flank. Simpson moves forward before spotting Tony Adcock's run into the box and then lofts a clever chip that leaves Adcock with just the keeper to beat and he does just that, managing to get over a high bounce and firing home from six yards out.

22 November 2008

Arsenal arrive at the Etihad Stadium with an impressive record against the Blues – the Gunners were one of those sides City rarely seemed to beat, but when Stephen Ireland scores in first-half injury time, things look promising. Then, seven minutes after the break, a moment of Brazilian magic. Shaun Wright-Phillips wins possession on the halfway line and then slips a through ball into Robinho's path – the Blues' record signing takes the pass in his stride and as keeper Manuel Almunia comes out, he calmly lifts the ball over his head for a sumptuous goal to double City's lead.

25 February 2012

Another poacher's goal for Sergio Aguero. A corner on the right is swung in by David Silva, Blackburn keeper Paul Robinson flaps at the cross and palms the ball down to Aguero who lashes it back past the former England keeper from eight yards to double City's lead on the day.

53

28 December 1981

Having beaten Liverpool 3-1 at Anfield on Boxing Day, another win would put City top going into the New Year. After a scrappy first period against Wolves ended 0-0, manager John Bond led his troops into the dressing room for a dressing down and, as a result, City re-emerged looking more focused and determined not to let the opportunity of leading the tightly packed First Division into the New Year pass them by. With only eight minutes of the second half gone, Asa Hartford drills home his second goal in three days to put the Blues 1-0 up.

1 April 1991

Crystal Palace defenders are asleep as Adrian Heath whips in a quick free kick from the right of the Eagles' box – he plays it into the six-yard box where Niall Quinn races in to head powerfully home from close range, completing his hat-trick and putting City 3-0 up at Selhurst Park.

9 September 2017

John Stones cuts out a Jordan Henderson pass and Fernandinho takes over, feeding a slide-rule pass through the middle for Sergio Aguero to chase on to, but this time the talisman City striker squares the ball to Gabriel Jesus who hits a left-foot shot into the net with keeper Simon Mignolet stranded to make it 3-0 for the Blues.

11 July 2020

City go 3-0 up away to Brighton & Hove Albion with Riyad Mahrez the architect as he sends in a superb cross from the right for Raheem Sterling to head home past Mat Ryan for his 26th goal of the campaign.

54

21 December 2011

Sergio Aguero's second of the afternoon and City's third on the night, this was another clinical finish from close range by the Argentinian. Gareth Barry finds Samir Nasri who plays a slide-rule ball across the box, flat-footing two Stoke City defenders before Aguero tucks home from six yards out to ensure City top the Premier League table at Christmas.

11 April 2012

As news filters through that Manchester United have gone behind to Wigan Athletic, Samir Nasri feeds a pass through to David Silva in the West Brom penalty area but it's Sergio Aguero who arrives first, steering an angled shot past Foster for his second of the night as the Blues claw back three points from United's lead in a pivotal night of the 2011/12 title race.

17 November 2012

A controversial penalty after the referee awards a spot kick for handball following David Silva's corner. The Aston Villa players complain long and loudly, but Sergio Aguero places the ball down and then coolly converts with a low shot past the keeper to double City's lead on the day.

9 April 2016

Holding his run until the perfect moment, Sergio Aguero latches on to a superbly weighted through ball from Samir Nasri before lashing a rising shot over Chelsea keeper Thibaut Courtois from eight yards out. A clinical finish from City's top scorer and a goal that puts the Blues 2-0 up at Stamford Bridge.

55

11 May 1985

City go 3-0 up against Charlton Athletic to place one foot firmly back in the top flight. Andy May sets Paul Power away down the left flank and his cross hangs in the air allowing Jim Melrose to send an improvised header past the teenage Addicks keeper and put the Blues 3-0 up.

28 August 2011

City go three goals up as Spurs' back line is again torn to shreds. The creator for the third is Yaya Toure who bursts into the box on the right before drilling a low cross into the six-yard box for Edin Dzeko to drill home, complete his hat-trick and put the Blues 3-0 up at White Hart Lane.

23 November 2013

City go 5-0 up against Spurs with less than an hour played as Manuel Pellegrini's men continue to run riot against the North Londoners. Yaya Toure plays a side pass to Fernandinho who then plays a ball to the feet of Alvaro Negredo on the edge of the box. The Spaniard spins off his marker before sending a thunderous shot past Hugo Lloris and into the top-right corner of the net.

2 March 2014

Trailing 1-0 to Sunderland in the Capital One Cup Final, City blow the Black Cats away with two goals in two minutes. After a frustrating first half, it's quickly evident that Manuel Pellegrini's men are determined to live up to their pre-match tag of overwhelming favourites and the goal that brings the Blues level is truly spectacular. Pablo Zabaleta brings the ball down the right before playing a pass inside to Yaya Toure who instinctively hits a curling shot from more than 30 yards out into the top-left corner of the Sunderland net. An incredible goal.

56

11 May 1985

Maine Road goes wild as City score again to make it 4-0 and all but secure promotion back to the top flight. Paul Simpson chases a long clearance towards the Charlton Athletic goal and as the young keeper hesitates, waiting for the ball to come into his area where he could collect, Simpson nips in and takes it around him before rolling the ball into the empty net.

2 March 2014

You wait for one spectacular goal to come along and then you get two in the space of a couple of minutes. Having just seen Yaya Toure level the scores against Sunderland in the Capital One Cup Final, Samir Nasri shows what he can do as Aleks Kolarov's cross falls at his feet and Nasri hits a curling, rising shot with the outside of his right boot that leaves the keeper motionless and puts City 2-1 up.

11 July 2020

City score a second goal in three minutes to go 4-0 up away to Brighton. It is a welcome goal for Bernardo Silva – his first in 20 Premier League games – but the Portuguese has Gabriel Jesus to thank after the Brazilian challenges a defender for the loose ball resulting from

Bernardo's low shot – and it is Bernardo who profits, tucking the ball home from close range.

57

27 November 1978

One of the best City goals ever scored in European football also puts the Blues 2-0 up in the San Siro Stadium against an AC Milan side who had never lost at home to an English team. In a hastily rearranged game played on a Thursday afternoon after fog had abandoned plans for the game the previous evening, Paul Power picked the ball up just outside his own area and then began a surge forward. Pretty much unchallenged, he continues to run for more than 60 yards down the right to the edge of the Milan box and fires in a weak shot that bobbles twice before deceiving Albertosi, nestling in the net to make it 2-0 to Tony Book's side in the UEFA Cup third round, first leg.

1 December 2010

Never has an opposition player received a reception quite like it! When Alan Douglas Borges de Carvalho enters the fray during City's Europa League meeting with Salzburg, he is introduced only as 'Alan' – and it is the start of a bizarre 35 minutes for the Brazilian. Cheering his every touch, jeering every time the officials gave a decision against him and chanting songs such as 'Alan is Superman', the City supporters got fully behind the Salzburg striker. Much to their disappointment,

Alan's only real chance of the game came to nothing – who knows what the reaction would have been if he'd scored! Still, a lasting bond was formed ...

58

23 September 1989

With City fans nervously biting their nails after Manchester United scored just after half-time, the Blues restore their three-goal advantage. Paul Lake bursts into the United box and forces a good save from Jim Leighton, but the ball is collected again by Lake who immediately squares a pass to the unmarked Oldfield to tap into the empty net and put City 4-1 up at Maine Road.

3 April 2010

City go 6-0 up away to Burnley as torrential rain threatens to wash the game away at Turf Moor. The Clarets' reputation of scoring from and defending set pieces is torn to shreds as they concede a third goal as a result of a left-wing corner; this time Vincent Kompany is the beneficiary, nodding past the keeper from six yards. Though the surface almost becomes unplayable, the referee allows the match to finish, with the Blues eventually winning 6-1.

17 September 2013

Proof Sergio Aguero is lethal with either foot – if needed – as he sweeps home a Champions League group-stage goal in the Czech Republic against Viktoria Plzen.

Samir Nasri plays in a short pass to Aguero in the box and, with his back to goal, he initially nudges the ball forwards before turning and lashing in a low left-foot shot with typical accuracy.

21 February 2017

Trailing 2-1 to Monaco in a crucial Champions League round of 16 first leg at the Etihad, City level the scores. Raheem Sterling spots Sergio Aguero's run, plays it into his path and Aguero hits a low shot that the Monaco keeper makes a terrible hash of and the ball ends up in the back of the net.

5 August 2018

Sergio Aguero puts City 2-0 up in the Community Shield clash with Chelsea at Wembley. John Stones starts the move as he intercepts a Chelsea attack on the edge of his own box before finding Ilkay Gundogan, Gundogan moves forward and plays it out right to Bernardo Silva who passes to Aguero in the box and he immediately sends a low drive past Willy Caballero to double the Blues' lead and secure victory for Pep Guardiola's trophy-hungry side.

59

11 August 2001

Kevin Keegan's first game as Manchester City manager was never going to be dull – Keegan didn't do dull. Played on a Saturday evening for live TV coverage, the Blues began their bid to bounce back to the top flight against Gianluca Vialli's Watford at Maine Road and in an electrically charged atmosphere, the Hornets rode their luck and held out until just before the hour-mark when Laurent Charvet picked up Berkovic's clever ball on the right and sent over a delicious cross for Goater to crash home a header and send Maine Road wild.

22 September 2001

In a see-saw game away to Sheffield Wednesday, City restore the lead. Ali Benarbia spots Danny Granville on the edge of the Owls box and he chests the ball into the feet of Shaun Goater who returns the favour, playing a short pass between two defenders and into Granville's path. The left-back finishes calmly from eight yards to put City 3-2 up – much to the delight of the 6,000 or so travelling Blues.

25 September 2010

Carlos Tevez enjoyed playing against Chelsea. He'd scored goals against them for West Ham, Manchester

United and City prior to this clash and adds another on this occasion. Chelsea's 100 per cent start meant they already had a seven-point advantage over City with just five games played so the Blues can ill-afford to lose any more ground so early in the campaign. City hold firm against the free-scoring Premier League leaders and, on 59 minutes, take the lead with a typically tenacious Tevez solo effort. The Argentine collects the ball around the halfway line and powers forward. Ashley Cole is brushed aside as the City striker nears the Chelsea goal and when he gets to within range he strikes a low shot across Petr Cech and into the net. The Etihad Stadium erupts as Tevez wheels away celebrating. It turns out to be the only goal of the game that put the Blues back in the hunt again.

19 May 2013

After a season of frustrating injuries, Jack Rodwell at least has a fine end to the season. Finally free of the hamstring problems that had blighted his first season at City, Rodwell shines in the last few games and scores twice in the last-day game against Norwich. His first is good but his second is even better, sprinting on to a Yaya Toure pass fully 50 yards before hitting a low shot past the Norwich keeper to make it 2-2.

10 December 2013

City level the scores in the Allianz Arena against Pep Guardiola's Bayern Munich. David Silva threads a pass to James Milner who races into the Germans' box only to be brought down by Dante. Aleks Kolarov coolly sends Manuel Neuer the wrong way to make it 2-2 in a thrilling Champions League group-stage clash.

25 January 2014

The first of a Sergio Aguero hat-trick against Watford, who had led 2-0 in the FA Cup fourth round at the Etihad. Stevan Jovetic finds Aleks Kolarov on the left and his low cross is turned goalwards by Edin Dzeko but the keeper makes a fine save, only for Aguero to poke home the rebound from close range – sparking a dramatic comeback by City.

60

7 March 1970

Trailing 1-0 to West Brom in the 1970 League Cup Final, City finally level the scores. Jeff Astle had opened the scoring after just six minutes, but gradually, Joe Mercer's side played their way back into the contest on a muddy, churned-up Wembley surface Mercer described as a 'pig of a pitch'. The goal comes when City win a corner on the hour-mark; Mike Summerbee flicks on the cross to Colin Bell who cushions a header into Mike Doyle's path and his first-time shot beats keeper John Osborne, and City, at last, are level.

11 May 1985

With just an hour played, City go 5-0 up against Charlton Athletic to seal promotion back to Division One. It is the third goal of a blistering five-minute spell and teenager Paul Simpson – already involved in three of the goals scored – is integral again as he chases Jim Melrose's ball out to the left, drives down the wing and his cross is laid off by Steve Kinsey to David Phillips who arrows a low shot into the bottom-right corner of the net from 20 yards to complete the rout at a sun-drenched Maine Road.

7 May 2000

A goal many felt would never come as City finally got their act together on a day they couldn't fail. Trailing

1-0 to Blackburn Rovers at Ewood Park, the home side – with little other than pride to play for – had struck the woodwork on FOUR occasions as promotion-chasing City rode their luck. The Blues needed a point to win back-to-back-promotions to the Premier League but were clinging on for dear life against Graeme Souness's side. Had any of those woodwork strikes gone in, Ipswich Town would have surely been promoted instead, but fortune was on the Blues' side and finally, the 15,000 City fans dotted around the ground had a goal to cheer when Kevin Horlock's superb left flank cross found Shaun Goater at the far post and the Goat did the rest, finishing from a few yards out to make it 1-1 and settle the nerves of players and fans alike.

28 August 2011

Samir Nasri plays a measured pass into the path of Sergio Aguero who picks up the ball on the left-hand side of the Spurs box. He drops his left shoulder and darts past defender Michael Dawson before thumping a left-foot shot high over Brad Friedel into the roof of the net for a superb individual effort that puts City 4-0 up at White Hart Lane. Explosive power, pace and strength – this goal has a bit of everything.

23 October 2011

With Manchester United reduced to ten men, City finally make the Reds pay by doubling the lead at Old Trafford – and it's the same trio responsible for the first goal who combine brilliantly again for the second. James Milner finds David Silva just inside the Reds' box and Silva waits until Milner races alongside him, plays the ball into his path and Milner's hard low cross finds an unmarked Mario Balotelli at the far post and he has the simple task of volleying home from close range to make it 2-0.

15 March 2012

City had surprisingly fallen 2-0 down to Sporting Lisbon in the Europa League round of 16 second leg at the Etihad. Already trailing 1-0 from the first leg, the Blues look down and out until Yaya Toure spots Sergio Aguero in space in the Lisbon box. He plays a short pass to his feet, the Argentine swings his right foot at the ball and sends a shot that gives Rui Patricio no chance.

6 November 2012

Trailing in a Champions League group-stage clash with Ajax but having halved the deficit, a long clearance forward finds the head of Mario Balotelli. The Italian striker nods the ball on and into the path of Sergio Aguero who takes a couple of paces before firing a low shot across the keeper and into the bottom left-hand corner from the edge of the box to make it 2-2 against the Dutch giants.

3 October 2015

Sergio Aguero bags his fourth this afternoon against Newcastle. David Silva again spots Kun in space, this time on the left, and he cuts inside one challenge before firing a right-foot shot low and hard past Tim Krul and into the bottom right-hand corner of the net. A superb finish from a striker at the very top of his game and the second time he'd hit four goals in one game for the Blues – but he still wasn't finished ...

5 March 2016

If Sergio Aguero's first goal against Aston Villa had been more than a shade fortunate, there is no luck about this wonderfully worked goal that begins with Aguero outside the box. He dinks the ball to David Silva who, in turn, lofts a pass over the defenders and into Kun's path. Aguero chests it down and then squeezes a shot past the keeper on his near post as City make it three goals in the space of 12 second-half minutes to make the score 3-0.

26 November 2016

Another scrappy goal for Sergio Aguero at Turf Moor but one that proves to be the winning goal against Burnley. As City look to go ahead for the first time in the game, Fernandinho salvages a ball that looks to be heading out before sliding a low cross into the six-yard box, where Aguero gleefully pokes home from close range for his second of the game and to put the Blues 2-1 up.

61

18 May 2019

Kevin De Bruyne puts City 3-0 up against Watford in the FA Cup Final at Wembley. Raheem Sterling sets Gabriel Jesus free and with just one defender and De Bruyne for company, he slides a pass to De Bruyne who dummies a shot, sending the keeper out of the equation, before taking his time to bury a low shot into the net and put the Blues 3-0 up.

62

5 May 1956

After being pegged back in the first half, City go 2-1 up in the 1956 FA Cup Final against Birmingham City. Jack Dyson is put clear after tremendous work by Don Revie, Bobby Johnstone and Ken Barnes and he makes no mistake, restoring City's lead with a composed finish.

3 August 1968

More terrible West Brom defending in the 1968 Charity Shield clash at Maine Road sees City go 5-1 up with barely an hour played. Mike Doyle's hopeful cross into the Baggies box suddenly becomes a good scoring chance for Neil Young as defender Doug Fraser completely misses his attempt at a headed clearance and Young makes no mistake with a typical rocket shot past the hapless sub keeper from a tight angle.

7 January 1978

A packed Elland Road and a war of the roses FA Cup third-round tie between two top sides of the day as Leeds United hosted City. Tony Book's side were definitely up for the cup in what was a hostile atmosphere inside the ground. City dominated much of the play but it wasn't until the 62nd minute that the Blues finally broke the deadlock. When Gordon McQueen fouls Brian Kidd on 62 minutes, Dave Watson lofts a free kick forward, Colin Bell bravely loops the ball on with his head and Dennis Tueart flings himself through a host of bodies to head high past keeper David Harvey. As the net bulges, the travelling army from Manchester go wild.

23 September 1989

One of the best Manchester derby goals ever scored, on a day when everything went City's way, seals the 111th clash of the Manchester clans. The move starts with Ian Bishop on the halfway line as he sprays an inch-perfect ball into the path of David White on the right flank. White immediately hits a superb cross into the box where it is met on the full by Andy Hinchcliffe who powers a header past the keeper to make it 5-1 with barely an hour of the game played. Though City fans dream of adding more misery, there will be no further scoring in what is a near-perfect 90 minutes for the Blues who register a first victory over United for 13 years.

24 February 1996

Georgi Kinkladze is at the heart of City's second goal against Newcastle United as he weaves in and out of challenges on a mesmeric run into the box before whipping in a low shot that Pavel Srnicek does well to keep out. The quick-thinking Kinkladze gathers the rebound and chips the ball perfectly to the far post for Niall Quinn to gleefully head home his fifth of the season and second of the game to give Alan Ball's side a 2-1 lead at Maine Road.

11 August 2001

A quite wonderful debut by Israeli playmaker Eyal Berkovic is capped by a superb goal. Having gone 1-0 up just a few minutes before, the Blues have their tails up and tear mercilessly at Watford's beleaguered rearguard, and when Paulo Wanchope crashes a header against the bar it is Berkovic who collects the rebound, cleverly moving the ball around Ramon Vega before planting it past Espen Baardsen for the second, killer goal. A wonderful goal by a very gifted player.

10 December 2013

City complete a stunning turnaround away to Bayern Munich. Having trailed 2-0 after just 12 minutes, City go 3-2 up at the Allianz Arena – and it is the same three players responsible for the first goal that are involved again as David Silva sets Jesus Navas away down the right flank and the Spaniard's cross eludes former City defender Jerome Boateng, lands at the feet of James Milner who then curls a beautiful shot in to give Manuel Pellegrini's side the lead. City will go close to getting the fourth goal needed to end as Group D winners, but Alvaro Negredo's late chance is saved by Manuel Neuer.

3 October 2015

A fifth goal in just 20 blistering minutes from Sergio Aguero. This goal was all about the vision of Kevin De Bruyne and the predatory instincts of Aguero. De Bruyne receives the ball but is facing away from goal when he pivots around to cross low into the six-yard box for Sergio to slide home from close range. An amazing spell of finishing by the Argentine that puts City 5-1 up against Newcastle United at the Etihad.

2 January 2017

A third successive goal against Burnley for Sergio Aguero – but not the completion of a hat-trick, as a quick turnaround of fixtures see the Clarets at the Etihad at the start of the New Year less than six weeks after the first meeting. If his brace against Burnley in the 2-1 win at Turf Moor had been untidy, this was anything but, as Raheem Sterling is felled in the box by goalkeeper Tom Heaton, Aguero carries on towards the loose ball before hitting a powerful shot from a tight angle past two defenders on the line and into the net. A super strike that puts ten-man City 2-0 up against Sean Dyche's side.

23 April 2017

Yaya Toure's long pass into the Arsenal half is controlled superbly by Sergio Aguero who speeds away from defender Nacho Monreal. He pushes the ball towards goal and as Petr Cech advances he calmly lifts it over the Gunners' keeper to put City ahead in the FA Cup semi-final at Wembley. It's just reward for Kun who had a perfectly good goal wiped out in the first half when the assistant referee wrongly deemed Leroy Sane's cross to have curled out of play momentarily. The Blues, however, let the lead slip and eventually lose 2-1 in extra time.

63

10 September 2011

Sergio Aguero's second goal of the afternoon comes after a sublime team move. Yaya Toure plays a short pass to David Silva who quickly flicks it to Samir Nasri on the edge of the box. The midfielder just reaches the ball in time to nutmeg a defender as he passes into Aguero's path and the Argentine makes no mistake with a low shot past Ali Al-Habsi to double the Blues' lead over Wigan Athletic.

23 February 2013

City were desperately looking for a breakthrough against Chelsea and it finally comes in the second half. David Silva manages to find Yaya Toure on the edge of the box and he cleverly drops his shoulder before curling a low shot past Petr Cech who was unsighted by a defender.

2 November 2014

In a tense Manchester derby at the Etihad, Sergio Aguero once again proves to be the match-winner. What will prove to be the only goal of the game comes when Yaya Toure plays a pass inside a United defender for Gael Clichy to run on to – the French left-back then pulls the ball back into the box and finds Aguero on the edge of the six-yard box and the City striker duly buries a left-foot shot powerfully past David De Gea from close range to secure a precious 1-0 victory for Manuel Pellegrini's side.

13 September 2017

John Stones caps a superb performance with his second goal of the evening to put City 4-0 up away to Feyenoord. The Dutch side hadn't learned their lesson after Stones's second-minute goal from a corner as the Blues' defender repeats the feat, this time nodding home Kevin De Bruyne's corner from close range to effectively end the contest at the De Kuip Stadium in Rotterdam.

12 May 2019

City at last get breathing space against Brighton at a sun-drenched Amex Stadium – and what a way to do it. Riyad Mahrez collects the ball 20 yards from goal, feigns a left-foot shot, leaving his marker on his backside before hitting a sweet right-foot shot into the top-right corner from the edge of the box to put the champions-elect 3-1 up on the south coast.

64

5 May 1956

City make it two goals in two minutes to stun Birmingham City in the 1956 FA Cup Final at Wembley. Bert Trautmann collects the ball and kicks long to Jack Dyson who flicks the ball on to Bobby Johnstone, who drills a low shot home to make it 3-1 and become the first player ever to score in consecutive Wembley finals in the process. It is also Johnstone's fourth of the competition and puts Les McDowall's side within sight of victory.

8 January 2012

City find themselves down to ten men and 3-0 behind by the break against Manchester United, just two months after thrashing the Reds 6-1 at Old Trafford. City fans fear the worst but Aleks Kolarov pulls one back early in the second half and just past the hour, Sergio Aguero meets a low cross on the full that David De Gea manages to keep out, but Kun is first to the loose ball and he makes no mistake from close range in a thrilling FA Cup third-round tie at the Etihad.

65

19 January 2010

One of the most memorable Manchester derby goals of modern times as Carlos Tevez puts City 2-1 up in the first leg of the Carling Cup semi-final against Manchester United. The Reds fail to clear a Craig Bellamy corner and, as the half-clearance is headed back into the danger area, Vincent Kompany hooks a short cross into the six-yard box where Tevez bravely gets between a defender and the keeper to nod the ball in from a couple of yards out to put City 2-1 up. It is the resulting celebration, however, that sticks in the memory as Tevez races to the halfway line, just in front of the Manchester United bench, putting his hands behind his ears as if to send a message to the club – and almost certainly to the manager – who didn't make his loan deal permanent.

17 May 2011

There was the danger of an 'after the Lord Mayor's Show' when City take on Stoke just three days after beating the Potters in the FA Cup Final. The Blues were on an unprecedented modern-day high following the 1-0 win at Wembley but there was still plenty of work to be done with a Champions League berth to confirm. But if the Potters thought they might be able to exact a modicum of revenge over City, Carlos Tevez had other ideas. Tevez, relishing his role as captain, puts the Blues ahead early on with a terrific goal on 14 minutes and Joleon Lescott adds a second shortly after the break. With City 2-0 up and coasting, the skipper pulls rank when a free kick was awarded some 30-plus yards out. It seemed a tad optimistic to say the least, but undeterred, Tevez runs up and powers a shot that initially swerves away from goal before bending back in and flying past the keeper into the top corner of the net. It was as good a free kick as you'll ever see and the mark of a gifted footballer.

11 November 2012

Trailing 1-0 to Spurs, City need inspiration to get back into the game – and it comes, just past the hour-mark. Carlos Tevez's attempted pass is cut out but Yaya Toure quickly wins back possession and diverts the ball into Sergio Aguero's path – he cuts the ball back inside as he heads into the box before expertly guiding a left-foot shot past the keeper to make it 1-1 at the Etihad.

10 May 2015

Sergio Aguero completes his fifth hat-trick for City. The goal that completes the treble comes from the penalty spot as he tucks away the spot kick after David Silva had been fouled in the box, putting the Blues 4-0 up on the day and on the way to a comprehensive 6-0 victory over QPR.

24 September 2016

When Kevin De Bruyne is fouled inside the Swansea City box, Sergio Aguero is given the chance to score his 11th goal of the season – while still only in September. With a variation of his usual technique, Aguero goes for a 'Panenka'-style spot kick and chips the ball down the middle as Lukasz Fabianski is easily beaten. The goal restores the Blues' lead and puts Pep Guardiola's side 2-1 up.

66

18 October 2014

Having missed a second penalty and then watched Spurs miss another, this crazy game sees the fourth penalty of the afternoon awarded on 66 minutes after Sergio Aguero is bundled over as he was about to turn home Jesus Navas's low cross. Aguero backs himself again and makes no mistake this time, completing his hat-trick and putting City 3-1 ahead.

2 July 2020

Already 3-0 up, City finally kill off the challenge of newly crowned Premier League champions Liverpool. Rodrigo digs a fine pass up to Kevin De Bruyne who cuts inside and then plays in Raheem Sterling on the right who sees his low drive helped home by Alex Oxlade-Chamberlain for what is later credited as an own goal.

67

7 November 1987

Paul Stewart puts City 6-0 up with an excellent header as Huddersfield Town continue to capitulate at Maine Road. Again, the provider is Paul Simpson who claims his third assist of the game with a wonderfully teasing left flank cross that Stewart meets on the corner of the six-yard box and loops his header over the keeper and into the far corner for his second of the afternoon.

7 May 2000

City get another huge slice of good fortune in the promotion decider at Ewood Park. Nicky Weaver's huge punt upfield is badly misjudged by Blackburn Rovers centre-half Christian Dailly and, not realising his keeper has come out to clear behind him, he heads the ball towards his own goal and realises in a split second where the ball is headed and, despite his desperate attempts to retrieve his error, he can't prevent an own goal and City go 2-1 up.

16 November 2012

If his first goal had been somewhat fortuitous against Aston Villa, Sergio Aguero's second of the game is excellent. Picking up the ball on the right, he drifts into the Villa penalty area before dropping his shoulder past the defender. He then fires a low shot under the keeper in a match that City go on to win 5-0.

11 March 2017

Leroy Sane dashes down the right flank, looks up and then whips the perfect low cross into the six-yard box where Sergio Aguero is most lethal and the Manchester City talisman makes no mistake with a smart finish from five yards out as City go 2-0 up away to Middlesbrough in the FA Cup sixth-round tie at the Riverside Stadium.

68

25 August 1923

It was a proud day for Manchester City and their fans as the Blues walked out into their brand new Moss Side home of Maine Road for the first time. A record home crowd of 56,993 packed in the new stadium with the club having left the less than grand surroundings of Hyde Road a few months earlier. Hosting Sheffield United, City and the Blades play out a goalless first half despite Tommy Johnson and Horace Barnes forcing the visitors' keeper Gough into a couple of decent saves. City come out for the second half determined to see off Sheffield United's challenge and the prestigious honour of the first ever goal scored at Maine Road goes to the prolific Barnes on 68 minutes after connecting with debutant Donaldson's cross.

7 November 1987

Two goals inside a minute for a rampant City side hungry for goals. Huddersfield Town's miserable day gets even worse as a defender receives a throw-in inside his own half, dithers and allows Tony Adcock to steal the ball and head into the box. Adcock cleverly runs across a retreating defender, knowing any contact will at least result in a penalty – but with no challenge he instead is free to clip the ball over the advancing keeper to complete his hat-trick and put City 7-0 up at Maine Road.

22 September 2001

City at last establish breathing space against Sheffield Wednesday as Paulo Wanchope bags his first goal of the game. The imperious Ali Benarbia is the creator, picking up a clearance from a throw-in just inside the Wednesday box before dinking a sublime chip that the Costa Rican glances home with his head to put Kevin Keegan's men 4-2 up at Hillsborough.

15 August 2011

Sergio Aguero announces his arrival at City with a predatory first goal for the club. Yaya Toure plays the ball to Micah Richards who races into the box before putting a low cross into the six-yard box and Aguero runs in to tap home at the far post. He was just nine minutes into his debut having come off the bench and the goal puts City 2-0 up against the Swans. Three minutes later, an acrobatic flick set up David Silva to make it 3-0 and City fans quickly realised they were watching the debut of a very special player.

16 January 2016

If Sergio Aguero's first goal of the afternoon had been a little fortunate, his second is anything but as a sweeping City move tears the Crystal Palace defence to shreds and ends as Kevin De Bruyne plays a simple pass to

Aguero, who only has to tap home from six yards out and make it 3-0.

18 May 2019

Game, set and match? It seems so as Gabriel Jesus bags his second of the game in the FA Cup Final against Watford. The Hornets, by now chasing a lost cause, are again caught on the counter-attack as Kevin De Bruyne sends Jesus clear and the young Brazilian keeps his cool to send a precise shot into the bottom-right of the Watford goal from 12 yards to make it 4-0 at Wembley.

69

7 November 1998

Having arrived on loan and marking a superb debut with a goal against Colchester United the week before, immediate fan favourite Andy Morrison scores the goal of his life as City take a 3-0 lead away to Oldham Athletic. Already two goals up in the third tier Greater Manchester derby at Boundary Park, the ball is partially cleared by the Latics' defence and bounced to Morrison who heads it to Shaun Goater who, in turn, nods it back to Morrison who instinctively hits a sweet left-foot volley into the top corner from 25 yards. Superb technique from the big centre-half. Needless to say, Joe Royle acts quickly to make Morrison's deal permanent and at £80,000, it turns out to be one of the smartest purchases City ever make.

4 February 2004

Game on? Surely not ... City were still trailing 3-1 and were a man down following Joey Barton's sending off but had somehow dug in at White Hart Lane to at least have a chance. What was needed was a second goal to really put the cat amongst the pigeons and, just before the 70-minute mark, it came. As the ball is cleared by the Spurs defence, it falls to Dutch midfielder Paul

Bosvelt, who hits a low drive that spins wickedly off Spurs defender Anthony Gardner and past Kasey Keller to make it 3-2. Suddenly the White Hart Lane crowd sounds anxious and the players respond accordingly, misplacing passes and looking increasingly nervous. Could City really do it?

10 September 2011

A goal created by the undoubted genius of David Silva. The Spaniard picks up the ball on the halfway line and quickly has three Wigan players around him. A clever drag back and piece of magic sees him wriggle free of his markers in a flash. He then spots Sergio Aguero's angled run in behind three Wigan defenders and plays a sublime pass through to leave Aguero with enough time to size up the keeper and roll the ball past him into the corner of the net to make it 3-0. It was Sergio's fifth goal in just 100 regulation minutes at the Etihad.

23 October 2011

City go 3-0 up at Old Trafford and yet again, United's weakness at left-back is exposed. Yaya Toure pings a pass to the feet of Mario Balotelli who lays a back-flick into the path of David Silva. Silva immediately releases the overlapping Micah Richards who races into the box and plays a precise low cross into the middle for Sergio Aguero to sweep home and put a more realistic slant on the scoreline.

25 August 2014

City are leading Liverpool by two goals when Sergio Aguero replaces Edin Dzeko on 68 minutes. Moments earlier, Jesus Navas had also come off the bench and the pair combine to devastating effect when Navas plays an inch-perfect pass in behind the Reds' defence from the right flank and into the path of Aguero. He tees himself up and then slips the ball past the keeper with only his second touch of the game.

24 February 2015

A real beauty from Sergio Aguero in the Champions League round of 16 clash at the Etihad. City are 2-0 behind to a Lionel Messi-inspired Barcelona side when Fernandinho plays a smart low ball to the edge of the box. David Silva's deft touch allows Aguero to take the ball on and fire a powerful shot past the keeper to halve the first-leg deficit and give the Blues a glimmer of hope to take back to the Nou Camp.

1 March 2017

A goal so typical of Sergio Aguero's scoring prowess – particularly in home games against Liverpool. Kevin De Bruyne's excellent low cross to the edge of the six-yard box is swept home by Aguero's right boot with precision to level the scores after the Blues had fallen behind to James Milner's 51st-minute penalty.

30 April 2017

Sergio Aguero knocks home another penalty with consummate ease after Leroy Sane was adjudged to have been fouled in the box. It puts City level at 1-1 with Middlesbrough at the Riverside – the hosts had gone ahead in the first half thanks to Aguero's former strike partner Alvaro Negredo.

1 November 2017

The goal that City fans had been waiting for. Sergio had endured a 0-0 draw with Wolves that he then scored in from the ensuing penalty shoot-out – though it didn't count towards his record – and had to watch the next game from the bench. It seemed he'd been poised forever on the cusp of history and with more than an hour of the Champions League clash with Napoli gone, many wondered whether he'd have to wait again to replace Eric Brook at the top of City's all-time scorers' list. Then, Fernandinho breaks out of defence and plays the perfect ball for Leroy Sane who powers through the Napoli defence on the halfway line and heads for goal. A fine last-ditch tackle foils the German winger but Aguero is first to react to the loose ball, collecting 30 yards out, and heads into the box with two defenders snapping at his heels before striking a precision shot from 18 yards past Pepe Reina to give the Blues a 3-2 lead, pass Eric Brook's record of 177 goals scored and forever write his name into the club's history books. A terrific goal from a fantastic player.

7 August 2020

City finally deservedly regain the lead over Real Madrid in the Champions League round of 16 second leg at the Etihad. The goal is entirely the result of the hard-working Gabriel Jesus who hounds Raphael Varane as he looks to deal with a long ball, gambles on a header back to Thibaut Courtois and then clips the ball past the Belgian from a tight angle. It puts City 2-1 up and 4-2 ahead on aggregate – a lead that won't be surrendered as the Blues move into the quarter-finals for the fourth time in club history.

70

4 October 1995

Martyn Margetson endured mixed success between the posts at Maine Road, but there are two games in particular which stick in the mind of most City supporters. City were away and cruising against Wycombe Wanderers when Margetson makes his one and only outfield appearance. Both outfield substitutes had already been used when Richard Edghill succumbed to injury, but the club had already prepared for such an eventuality. Tony Book runs down the tunnel and returns with a blue shirt with 'MARGETSON' on the back; the City stopper proceeds to play the remaining 20 minutes in the unfamiliar role of centre-forward. Luckily, goals from Niall Quinn, Keith Curle and a brace from Uwe Rosler ensured that Margetson had a largely uneventful (if tiring!) spell up front.

22 September 2001

Two goals in the space of three minutes wrap up the points for City who go 5-2 up away to Sheffield Wednesday. The fifth is scored by the prolific Shaun Goater but it is again the brilliance of Ali Benarbia that creates the chance. After Danny Tiatto's cross is cleared back to the Australian, he plays a short ball to Benarbia on the edge of the box and the Algerian then threads an eye of the needle pass into Goater's clever run and the City striker nips in ahead of the keeper and rolls home his second of the game from a tight angle.

6 May 2012

Amid unbearable tension at St James' Park, City at last break through against Newcastle United. It was a game City had to win if the title had any chance of coming back to the blue half of Manchester for the first time in 44 years – the Blues needed six points from their final two matches. In this, City's penultimate game, Roberto Mancini's side were up against an excellent Newcastle outfit that needed three points to continue their challenge for Champions League football, so this was one of the last places the Blues wanted to visit. But with the score still 0-0 with 70 minutes played, City finally get the breakthrough via their big-game specialist Yaya Toure. Nigel de Jong and Sergio Aguero play their part and it is the latter who plays a one-two with Toure who unleashes a low curling drive from more than 20 yards out to put the Blues 1-0 up.

11 February 2015

David Silva makes the goal that puts City 3-1 up away to Stoke. Silva's dogged determination sees him spin from his marker in the box before being felled from behind as he moves away. Sergio Aguero makes no mistake from the spot with a low shot into the bottom right-hand corner to all but finish off the Potters.

12 August 2017

City had to be patient against Premier League newcomers Brighton on the opening day of the 2017/18 campaign. The Seagulls, buoyed by a passionate home crowd at the Amex Stadium, hold firm until the Blues finally make the breakthrough as David Silva slots a ball in to Sergio Aguero in the box and his powerful shot across the keeper puts City in command – at last.

6 May 2019

With City needing to win their game in hand to finally move above Liverpool in the Premier League table, the clock is ticking against a determined and resolute Leicester City. When skipper Vincent Kompany picks up the ball midway inside the Foxes half, he pushes it forward and the general consensus is – please don't shoot, Vinny! – but he does, unleashing a 25-yard howitzer that rockets into the top-left corner to give Kasper Schmeichel no chance and secures a crucial 1-0 win for the Blues with one game to play ...

71

6 April 1996

City were well and truly up against it. The relegation battle had begun as early as October as Alan Ball's side made a terrible start to the 1995/96 campaign and were rooted to the foot of the table with more than a third of the season gone. Worse still, neighbours Manchester United were powering their way towards the title and knew a Manchester derby win at Maine Road would further deepen the gloom surrounding the club. The match went to form early on with Eric Cantona giving United the lead, but City level through Mikhail Kavelashvili before the break – only to concede again almost immediately after the restart. The signing of Kavelashvili meant Uwe Rosler is relegated to the subs' bench, despite being one of City's more reliable performers. It seemed there was needle between the German striker and Ball, but few realised how deep that feeling ran until Rosler, now off the bench, equalises. Picking up the ball on the right, he cuts inside and unleashes his anger and frustration with a ferocious low drive from 20 yards that gives Peter Schmeichel no chance. Rosler waved his team-mates away as he points to the name on his back as he sends his manager a message in a demonstration of defiance. It was also a cracker of a goal.

5 May 1996

Trailing 2-0 to Liverpool and needing a win to stay up, City are thrown a lifeline when Neil Ruddock scythes down Georgi Kinkladze and the referee awards a penalty. Uwe Rosler steps up to power the ball past David James to give the Blues hope of a late comeback against the Reds.

2 October 2005

In what was the earliest kick-off time on record for the club, City host Everton in a Sunday morning 11.15am kick-off. With breakfast still heavy on the stomach and one or two bleary eyes among the City of Manchester Stadium crowd, the game began with neither City nor Everton ripping up trees during the 2005/06 season and it's fair to say that there is a fairly subdued atmosphere in the early autumnal sunshine. The Toffees, bottom of the Premier League, and City plodding along in mid-table added to a surreal feeling surrounding the game with a distinct lack of quality on show. It was proving to be a forgettable affair until a goal worthy of a much grander occasion. With 71 minutes played, full-back Danny Mills had the ball at his feet on the right flank. Of the few shots he'd managed in his City career, most had troubled those sat in Row Z rather than the opposition goalkeeper, but this time, things would be different. Mills cuts inside one challenge and then lets fly with a 25-yard howitzer that flies like a missile into the top corner, giving Nigel

Martyn no chance whatsoever and putting City on the way to a 2-0 win.

2 November 2013

Already 5-0 up against Norwich City at the Etihad, the visitors' afternoon is about to get even worse as David Silva's low ball from the left is only half-cleared by the Canaries' defence and Sergio Aguero is on hand to lash the ball home from eight yards and make it 6-0.

3 December 2014

Having trailed earlier in the game, City complete an impressive recovery by going 4-1 up away to Sunderland. The goal that puts the game beyond doubt comes when James Milner's low cross is turned home by Sergio Aguero from seven yards out via the post for his second goal of the night and his 19th of (yet another) prolific campaign.

21 February 2017

In a thrilling clash with Monaco at the Etihad, two teams hell-bent on attacking and entertaining fans continue to swap punches. Trailing 3-2 and with the clock ticking, City make it 3-3 as Sergio Aguero never takes his eye off David Silva's deep corner before planting a beautiful volley past the keeper to make the score 3-3 in a breathtaking Champions League round of 16 first leg at the Etihad.

72

7 January 1978

With City 1-0 up away to Leeds United in the FA Cup third round and the clock ticking down, the hosts are forced to gamble and leave gaps at the back in a bid to find an equaliser. But in an open, entertaining game, it is City who score next with 18 minutes to go; as Willie Donachie crosses from the left, Colin Bell gets up above Frank Gray to head powerfully towards goal – keeper David Harvey mistimes his jump slightly, pushes the ball up on to the bar and, as players rush in on the loose ball, Peter Barnes gets a toe-end to it from close range to put City 2-0 up.

19 November 2011

When Micah Richards is felled in the box by Hatem Ben Arfa, Sergio Aguero collects the ball and places it on the spot. Mario Balotelli had already scored a penalty earlier in the game but had been substituted so Aguero steps up and calmly slots the ball to Tim Krul's left to put City 3-0 up against the previously unbeaten Magpies.

6 April 2016

City level the scores away to PSG with a crucial second goal. Probing for an equaliser, Jesus Navas waits for support before nudging the ball to his right where Bacary

Sagna then sends in a low ball that PSG fail to clear and Fernandinho hits a deflected shot that bobbles into the bottom-left corner of the net from close range to make it 2-2 at the Parc des Princes.

3 January 2019

Leroy Sane scores the goal that will beat Liverpool 2-1 at the Etihad in a crucial top-of-the-table clash. Raheem Sterling plays the ball to Sane who races towards the edge of the box before unleashing a low left-foot shot across Alisson and in off the right-hand post to put the Blues ahead. The victory will see Liverpool's lead at the top reduced to just four points.

12 May 2019

The icing on the cake and the goal that sparks wild celebrations in the stand behind the goal as City go 4-1 up in the final game of the 2018/19 campaign. Ilkay Gundogan is the scorer, floating a curling free kick over the wall and into the top-right corner to give the Blues a 14th straight victory and ensure back-to-back Premier League titles – the first club to do so for ten years.

73

5 May 1956

With 17 minutes remaining and City 3-1 up in the FA Cup Final at Wembley, Birmingham's Peter Murphy outpaces Dave Ewing in the City box. Goalkeeper Bert Trautmann bravely dives at the feet of Murphy, but in the collision, Murphy's right knee hits Trautmann's neck with force. Trautmann is knocked unconscious and the referee stops play immediately. City trainer Laurie Barnett rushes on to the pitch, and treatment continues for several minutes. With no subs allowed at that time, City would have to see out the game with ten men if Trautmann was unable to continue. Captain Roy Paul was convinced Trautmann was not fit to complete the match and suggested Roy Little go in goal for the remaining minutes. However, Trautmann, dazed and unsteady on his feet, insists on remaining in net and after a lengthy delay, the game continues. Trautmann, in great pain, has two saves to make with City doing all they can to protect him by launching the ball anywhere in the time that remained. Trautmann collides with Dave Ewing in one attack, leaving him in even more agony – X-rays will later reveal the injury could have resulted in permanent paralysis! City see the game out, winning 3-1, and Trautmann's bravery became the stuff of legend – though it could have ended tragically for the big German keeper who would eventually make a full recovery and go down in history as the goalkeeper who played on despite having broken his neck.

21 November 2012

Trailing to a tenth-minute Karim Benzema goal, Sergio Aguero wins and converts the penalty that draws City level with Real Madrid. After being fouled in the box, Kun sends the keeper the wrong way from the spot but the draw isn't enough for the Blues who are eliminated from the competition as a result.

15 January 2014

A fairly simple goal by Sergio Aguero's lofty standards in an FA Cup third-round replay at home to Blackburn Rovers. Edin Dzeko moves forward and then plays a simple pass to his strike partner who pushes the ball to his left before firing a low shot from inside the box to put City 4-0 up on the night.

1 March 2017

Raheem Sterling sends a clever ball towards the six-yard box from the right flank and Sergio is on to it like a flash, turning the ball home with a rising shot from the right to finally kill off a lively Huddersfield Town side and book a place in the FA Cup quarter-finals for Pep Guardiola's side.

74

4 May 1968

A tiring City, clinging on to a crucial 2-0 lead that would leave the Blues just one more win away from a first top-flight title in 31 years, dig deep to punish Tottenham one more time. A monumental first-half effort had taken its toll on City who were now under intense pressure at White Hart Lane. A goal for Spurs and it's likely the home side would have gone and scored another one or maybe two goals, but showing the true grit of champions, City break and Mike Summerbee makes no mistake to make it 3-0 at White Hart Lane – it was perfect timing from Buzzer and though Jimmy Greaves would pull a goal back from the penalty spot on 83 minutes, City saw out the time that remained and began to focus on the title decider at Newcastle just a week away.

6 October 2012

David Silva starts the move that leads to the Blues doubling their lead against Sunderland. The Spaniard plays a pass to Aleks Kolarov on the left flank and the Serbian fires in a low cross that Aguero runs on to and lashes home from six yards out with perfect timing.

13 February 2013

Sergio Aguero's second of the afternoon comes courtesy of a superb piece of vision by David Silva. The playmaker holds the ball up on the right before lofting a clever ball over the Leeds defence for Aguero to run on to and finish with a low shot off the post to complete a 4-0 rout for the Blues.

1 November 2016

City wrap up a famous 3-1 win over Barcelona having gone close numerous times to adding to their lead previously. The third of a memorable evening comes when Kevin De Bruyne finds Jesus Navas on the right and the pacey winger moves into the box, crosses into the middle where a diving Sergio Aguero actually deflects the ball behind him with his shoulder – but the ball falls perfectly for Ilkay Gundogan to lash home from six yards. It is the German's second of the night and will be enough to ensure City record a first win over the Catalans in six attempts.

75

26 December 1981

City are awarded a penalty and the chance to go 2-0 up away to Liverpool with just 15 minutes left. A long Joe Corrigan punt upfield causes confusion in the Reds' defence and a mixture of Phil Thompson and Bruce Grobbelaar sees the ball fall to Steve Kinsey at the edge of the box and his powerful shot is tipped over – by central defender Thompson! The referee points to the spot and Kevin Bond keeps his cool to double the Blues' lead with his first goal for the club.

7 May 2000

Breathing space and time to start celebrating? That's not a City fan's style! After watching a torturous first hour, City come from 1-0 down and many, many Blackburn Rovers near misses to go 3-1 up. Paul Dickov is the target for a cross from the right but the ball eventually falls at the feet of Mark Kennedy who all but seals promotion with a sweet low left-foot finish before running off to celebrate with manager Joe Royle.

14 September 2011

Pitted in the fabled 'Group of Death', City's first ever Champions League match against Napoli begins a new chapter in the club's history. The Blues can't start with a victory, however, with Aleksandar Kolarov having the honour of scoring City's first goal in the competition, curling a superb free kick over the wall and into the net to earn a 1-1 draw against the Italians.

14 April 2012

Sergio Aguero's second of the afternoon comes as he carries the ball into the Norwich box before cutting inside and lifting a clever shot over the diving Ruddy into the far corner as the Blues head for a second 6-1 win on the road this campaign at Carrow Road.

18 October 2014

Sergio Aguero grabs his fourth goal of the game and completes a memorable afternoon with a terrific solo effort as he dashes towards the right-hand side of the Spurs box chasing a Fernandinho pass before checking inside on to his left foot and hitting a low shot into the bottom left-hand corner of the net to complete a memorable day and a 4-1 win for City.

76

12 April 2016

Kevin De Bruyne scores the goal that puts City in the Champions League semi-final. Having drawn 2-2 in the first leg, City and PSG again go hammer and tongs in the quarter-final second leg at the Etihad and both sides should have scored earlier. Sergio Aguero had missed a first-half penalty and the visitors had seen a goal chalked off for offside before De Bruyne finally broke the deadlock. Collecting the ball on the edge of the PSG box, the Belgian nudges it inside before rasping a low right-foot shot into the bottom corner to make it 1-0 and seal a win that takes Manuel Pellegrini's Blues further in the Champions League than ever before.

77

14 September 2016

Sergio Aguero completes yet another hat-trick against Borussia Monchengladbach to put City 3-0 up in the Champions League group-stage clash. Aguero chases on to a clever Raheem Sterling pass inside the full-back, drawing the keeper off his line, before nudging the ball to the left and rolling it into the empty net.

21 February 2017

City go back in front having twice trailed against Monaco in the Champions League round of 16 first leg. Monaco, having failed to learn from City's third goal which resulted from a David Silva corner from the right, conceded a second in six minutes, this time from a corner on the left. Kevin De Bruyne whips a curling cross in and Yaya Toure's near-post flick allows John Stones to slide home at the far post from a couple of yards out to make it 4-3 on the night.

9 September 2017

Leroy Sane climbs off the bench to put City 4-0 up against Liverpool at the Etihad. The young German winger had only been on the pitch for 20 minutes when he plays a smart one-two with Benjamin Mendy who sends a low cross towards the edge of the six-yard box and Sane makes no mistake with a low shot past Simon Mignolet and just inside the post.

78

24 February 1996

In a pulsating clash with Newcastle United, City go back in front for the third time as Steve Lomas crosses into the box from the right wing and Uwe Rosler steers home his sixth of the campaign with only 14 minutes to go and makes it 3-2 against the title-chasing Magpies. Maine Road erupts, but depressingly, it would be the only time that season that the Blues managed to score more than two goals.

5 May 1996

City fans start to believe as Kit Symons levels to make it 2-2 against Liverpool. With Alan Ball's side needing to better Coventry and Southampton's final day result, the Blues score a second in seven minutes when Martin Phillips's cross into the box is half-volleyed past David James at pace to level the score at Maine Road. Incredibly, with the other two games both drawing as well, only a win will save City but confusion as to what's needed ends up with Steve Lomas wasting time in the corner, believing City had done enough – they hadn't and, after an urgent message is relayed that a draw is not enough, City find they have run out of time and are relegated from the Premier League as a result.

21 March 2012

With City desperate to close the gap on leaders United, losing at home to Chelsea isn't an option. Yet, with time running out, Gary Cahill's goal on the hour-mark separates the teams. Then, Pablo Zabaleta's shot is handled in the box by Michael Essien and Aguero steps up to calmly slot home his 24th goal of the season and put the Blues level before Samir Nasri's late winner keeps City's title ambitions on track.

3 February 2013

This was undoubtedly one of Sergio Aguero's best goals for City and it was just a pity it wasn't the winner as this was a goal worthy of settling any game. City had earlier led 1-0, but Liverpool came back with two goals to lead 2-1 and, when Aguero chases a hopeful ball towards the Liverpool corner flag, there seemed little on for the Argentine. But Pepe Reina's rash decision to chase the ball to the side of his box allows Aguero to nudge it past the Reds' keeper and pivot a shot from a seemingly impossible angle in off the underside of the crossbar to earn City a 2-2 draw. An incredible goal from an incredible striker.

8 April 2013

The title might have been a lost cause but City still had plenty of pride to play for. A stunning goal that is all about the power and strength Sergio Aguero possesses. With the scores level at Old Trafford against Manchester

United, Aguero picks up the ball outside the United box, powers past four challenges before sending an arrowed shot into the top corner from the edge of the six-yard box to secure another memorable Old Trafford victory and send the travelling City fans wild.

25 January 2014

When Stevan Jovetic passes to Sergio Aguero midway inside the Watford half, there seems little threat, but Aguero darts forward, cuts inside a defender's challenge before curling a beautiful shot with his left foot into the top corner from 18 yards out to bring City level at 2-2 in the FA Cup fourth-round tie at the Etihad.

27 January 2016

A stunning goal that edges City to the Carabao Cup Final at Wembley. Having at one stage trailed 3-1 on aggregate to Everton in the semi-final second leg at the Etihad, the Blues claw their way back to 2-1 on the night and 3-3 on aggregate. Then, Kevin De Bruyne whips in a superb cross towards the penalty spot and Sergio Aguero cleverly guides a powerful header past the keeper by allowing the pace of the ball to do the hard work – a fantastic goal that lifts the roof off the Etihad and secures a 3-1 win over the Toffees.

16 August 2016

After neat work by Nolito and Kevin De Bruyne, Sergio Aguero effectively puts the Champions League play-off tie out of Steaua's reach in the first leg as Nolito eventually plays a short pass to his right in the box for Aguero to fire past the keeper and put City 4-0 up.

79

22 September 2001

City complete a 6-2 victory away to Sheffield Wednesday as Kevin Keegan's side show how devastating they can be on their day. The sixth goal of a mouth-watering attacking display comes when Richard Dunne cleverly shakes off a challenge deep inside his own half and then plays a 60-yard pass that releases Darren Huckerby to race clear – as he's about to pull the trigger, he is felled in the box and Paulo Wanchope hammers the resulting penalty high into the middle of the net to cap a memorable day in the Steel City.

18 January 2014

Collecting a short pass from Jesus Navas 30 yards out, Aguero carries the ball forward into the Cardiff box before jinking left, then right and thumping the ball home having tormented the Bluebirds' defender in the process. The goal puts City 4-1 up at the Etihad.

23 September 2017

The goal that puts Sergio one shy of Eric Brook's record total of 177. Leroy Sane whips in a curling cross and the accuracy is such Sergio needs to only guide a header low and past the Crystal Palace goalkeeper from seven yards out, having not had to adjust his feet at all, as City go 4-0 up against Roy Hodgson's side.

26 February 2020

City trail 1-0 to Real Madrid in the round of 16 Champions League first leg at the Bernabeu when, deservedly, the scores are levelled. Raheem Sterling and De Bruyne exchange passes and the Belgian's cross just clears the head of Sergio Ramos and finds Gabriel Jesus who heads past Thibaut Courtois to make it 1-1 and give the Blues a crucial away goal.

80

7 November 1987

City go 8-0 up – fittingly on 80 minutes – with a goal that is almost too easy. With Huddersfield Town's defending bordering on shambolic, Tony Adcock threads a ball through to Andy Hinchcliffe who races clear into the box unchallenged before unselfishly sliding the ball across to Paul Stewart to complete his hat-trick from close range.

4 February 2004

The 1,500 or so City fans that had made the journey to White Hart Lane for an FA Cup replay with Spurs roar on their ten-man team who had come back from 3-0 down to make it 3-2 – but it was about to get a whole lot better. With ten minutes to go, Shaun Wright-Phillips is put clear through and as keeper Kasey Keller races off his line, the City winger lifts the ball gently over him to make it 3-3. It was a fantastic comeback by Kevin Keegan's struggling side and even if Spurs had gone on and grabbed a winner, it proved the team were capable of much better things – but there was still one more twist to come ...

12 September 2009

Sometimes players are criticised for not celebrating goals passionately enough, but that certainly wasn't the case as Emmanuel Adebayor scores during the Blues' 4-2 win over his former club Arsenal. The Togolese striker leaps to meet a cross and plants a superb header past Manuel Almunia to give City a 3-1 lead at the Etihad – but his celebration sees him run from one box to another, sliding on his knees in front of the furious Arsenal fans who had jeered him all game. It earns Adebayor a yellow card, but he didn't seem to mind that much!

19 October 2013

City seal three points with a stunning goal away to West Ham United. Yaya Toure plays a low ball to Sergio Aguero who collects the pass and darts into the Hammers' box but instead of shooting, he back-heels the ball into the path of David Silva who feigns one shot before curling a left-foot shot into the top-left corner of the Hammers' net to make it 3-1. A wonderful goal.

9 April 2016

Yet another Sergio Aguero hat-trick as City go 3-0 up away to Chelsea. When Fernandinho is fouled by keeper Thibaut Courtois, the home keeper is shown a straight red card, and sub Asmir Begovic's first job is to collect the ball out of the net after Aguero sends him the wrong way to complete his hat-trick – perhaps his most impressive yet.

15 April 2017

With City in the middle of a rampant passage of play, Kevin De Bruyne somehow digs a superb cross in from the right of the Southampton box and Sergio Aguero simply wants it more than the home defenders as he heads home from close range to put the Blues 3-0 up at St Mary's.

81

27 April 1974

With Tommy Docherty's Manchester United in freefall towards Division Two, after a remarkable career at Old Trafford, 34-year-old Denis Law is enjoying a last hurrah with City – the club he left some 13 years earlier. Law had been signed on a free transfer from the Reds by then-manager Johnny Hart but nothing could have prepared the prolific Scot – or City – for the drama that was in store in this famous Manchester derby. In what was the penultimate game of a nightmare season for United, with just nine minutes left, Law instinctively back-heels Francis Lee's square ball past United home keeper Alex Stepney to hand City a 1-0 win. As the enormity of the moment dawned on both Law and a stunned crowd of 56,966, a crestfallen Law is inconsolable as he walks back to the centre circle having rubber-stamped his old club's relegation. It will be the last kick in league football of Law's career.

7 May 2000

The icing on the cake that starts the party in earnest at Ewood Park. Just as he had done 12 months before, Paul Dickov scores City's last goal of the season from open play and, while not quite as dramatic as his last-gasp effort against Gillingham, it was just as enjoyable as the diminutive Scot races through on goal, holding off a challenge before slotting past the keeper to seal a 4-1 win over Blackburn Rovers and confirm automatic promotion back to the Premier League for Joe Royle's side.

23 January 2016

Trailing 2-1 away to West Ham United, City press for a late equaliser. Kelechi Iheanacho is tackled on the edge of the Hammers box, but the ball only falls into the path of Sergio Aguero who makes no mistake from seven yards out with a confident finish – his second of the game – and earns City a 2-2 draw.

16 September 2017

One of Sergio Aguero's best for City? Definitely, maybe! Kyle Walker knocks the ball in with a short pass from the right and Aguero does the rest, gliding past one, two, three and then a fourth Watford defender before sliding his third of the game past Heurelho Gomes to complete a superb hat-trick. It is a quite breathtaking individual goal that his son Benjamin's grandfather, Diego Maradona, would be proud of! It also means he has scored five goals against Watford in the past two meetings – just six games apart – as rampant City go 5-0 up at Vicarage Road.

18 May 2019

Raheem Sterling finally gets his name on the scoresheet after a stellar display by the City forward. Bernardo is the creator, bursting past two challenges on the left of the Watford box before crossing into the six-yard box for Raheem Sterling to side-foot the ball high into the roof of the net to make it 5-0 in the FA Cup Final.

11 July 2020

Raheem Sterling completes his hat-trick as City go 5-0 up away to Brighton. It's a bizarre headed goal, too, as Sterling chases a high pass into the box then knocks it over a defender's head – but then starts to tumble as he nears the keeper and the ball comes down, hits the top of his head, goes through the goalkeeper's legs and, despite a despairing attempt to clear by a defender, crosses the line.

7 August 2020

David Silva makes his final appearance as a City player at the Etihad as he comes on to replace Raheem Sterling. The fact that such a wonderful talent and Club legend has to play his last game in front of an empty stadium is almost cruel. One can only imagine the reception he would have got as he came on for one last game on home soil – and though he will no doubt return in the future when fans fill the Etihad, it was a real pity that they couldn't have been present as City beat Real Madrid 2-1 to move into the Champions League quarter-finals.

82

15 March 2012

This goal sets up a grandstand finish as City come from 2-0 down at home to Sporting Lisbon in the Europa League to lead 3-2 on the night, level the aggregate scores at 3-3 but still trail on the away-goals rule. Aleks Kolarov's corner finds the head of Edin Dzeko who gets enough contact to divert the ball towards the lurking Aguero who hooks a volley in from close range to put the Blues ahead. But for a great late save, Blues keeper Joe Hart sees a header come within a whisker of winning the game for City who eventually run out of time and exit the competition a few seconds later.

21 February 2017

City's fifth goal of the game and arguably the best of the lot. Yaya Toure starts the move with a short pass to Sergio Aguero who, in turn, finds David Silva on the edge of the box – with a wall of defenders ahead of him, Silva lifts a clever pass into the path of Aguero who unselfishly lays the ball to his right for Leroy Sane to roll into the empty net and put City 5-3 up against Monaco in the Champions League round of 16 first leg at the Etihad.

83

29 November 2011

City hadn't won away to Arsenal for 36 years, but Sergio Aguero's late goal puts an end to the long barren run. With the score 0-0 in this League Cup quarter-final at the Emirates, Edin Dzeko's excellent run and cross-field pass eventually finds its way to Aguero who nudges the ball forward before he rifles a low shot past Lukasz Fabianski into the bottom corner to send the Blues into the semi-finals.

17 April 2013

With Wigan Athletic stubbornly holding on for a draw – and looking likely to maybe even snatch a shock win – Carlos Tevez pops up with a winning goal with just minutes remaining. Collecting a pass from Aleks Kolarov just outside the box, Tevez shields the ball and then wriggles past two challenges before hitting a shot high into the top corner from 15 yards out to secure a 1-0 win for City.

27 April 2013

The theory that Yaya only scores spectacular or important goals for City is underlined by this peach of a shot. The Ivorian picks up the ball on the edge of the West Ham United box and drifts in a few yards before firing a curling shot into the top left-hand corner that the Hammers keeper has no chance of stopping to give the Blues a much-needed cushion at 2-0.

8 November 2014

Another great Sergio Aguero goal out of nothing earns City a 2-2 draw away to QPR. Yaya Toure lofts a superb pass into the path of the Argentine who chests the ball down and knocks it around the keeper before stopping the ball with his right foot and then planting the ball into the net with his left.

26 February 2020

Having equalised just four minutes earlier in the round of 16 Champions League first leg, City take the lead and super sub Raheem Sterling is once again heavily involved as he streaks into the Real Madrid box only to be felled by Dani Carvajal. The referee points to the spot and Kevin De Bruyne makes no mistake with a low shot into the bottom left-hand corner with 83 minutes played to complete a superb turnaround and score what will be a famous winning goal at the Bernabeu.

84

7 March 1981

Trailing 2-1 in the FA Cup quarter-final away to Everton, City keep the Wembley dream alive with a late equaliser at Goodison Park. A classic City build-up down the left saw two separate one-twos played between Kevin Reeves and Steve Mackenzie and then Mackenzie and Paul Power. Power, who had run tirelessly all afternoon, digs deep, and finds the energy to reach the edge of the Everton box before scooping a tired right leg at the ball, just as Mick Lyons comes thundering in with his challenge. The ball sails high over the onrushing Toffees keeper Jim McDonough and seems to hang for an eternity before dropping down and into the back of the net. The celebrations began behind the goal at the Park End with more than 10,000 delirious City fans as Power was swamped by team-mates and a 2-2 draw secured.

16 February 2012

With the clock running down and City drawing 1-1 in the Europa League first leg against FC Porto, second-half sub Sergio Aguero arrives to swing the tie City's way. In a move that starts with Yaya Toure and Samir Nasri playing a one-two, the Ivorian powers into the box before squaring the ball for Aguero to tap home from six yards out.

2 January 2016

City had trailed 1-0 to Watford but managed to get on level terms shortly before Sergio Aguero's goal. Bacary Sagna's deep cross into the box finds the head of Aguero, who almost hangs in the air before nodding a well-placed header just out of the reach of Heurelho Gomes for a dramatic late winner.

85

28 December 1981

Level with Wolves at 1-1 and needing a win to go top, City desperately push for a late winner. With five minutes to go, Trevor Francis, largely anonymous throughout the match, shows why City had splashed out more than a million pounds on his undoubted match-winning qualities. Joe Corrigan launches a mighty clearance into the Wolves half and defender George Berry can only direct his header into Francis's path. Francis takes a half a dozen steps forward before lashing a thunderous drive into the back of the net from the edge of the box. Maine Road erupts and this time the Blues hold out in the final nervous moments to win 2-1. The celebrations at the final whistle were testament enough to how the City fans felt about topping the table for the first time in four years.

7 November 1987

With five minutes remaining, Huddersfield Town – 8-0 down already – still hadn't worked out that playing a high line against City's pacey attack was not working and Neil McNab is again able to play through the ragged back four to free Tony Adcock. Adcock races down the right and crosses low into the box where the ball is partially cleared – but only as far as David White who races in to drill the loose ball home and put City 9-0 up with five minutes to go.

23 March 1988

City had been stunned by Chelsea's response to going behind in the Full Members' Cup Final at Wembley. Goals from David Speedie (3) and Colin Lee (2) had seemingly wrapped up a comprehensive 5-1 win for Chelsea with just five minutes remaining – but City launched an astonishing fightback in the last few moments. Paul Simpson's fine cross from the left flank finds the head of Mark Lillis who guides his header into the top-right corner to pull one back for the Blues who still trail 5-2.

23 February 2013

Though Yaya Toure's goal had put City 1-0 up, Chelsea are still well in the game and looking for an equaliser, so when sub Carlos Tevez picks up a pass from David Silva 25 yards out, he takes one look up before hitting a cracking shot past Petr Cech to seal a deserved 2-0 win for the Blues.

21 September 2014

Frank Lampard had played 648 times for Chelsea and scored 211 goals during a 13-year stay with the club, yet now he was facing the team whose supporters regarded him as a modern-day legend in the sky blue colours of City. Lampard had put his move to New York City FC on hold while he had one last hurrah in the Premier League and it was always going to be an emotional moment to face his old club. City were stuttering in their defence of the Premier League title while Chelsea arrived at the Etihad with a 100 per cent record from their opening four games.

In what was a tightly contested game of few opportunities the odds tip in the visitors' favour when Pablo Zabaleta is sent off for clashing with Diego Costa, and Andre Shurrle put Chelsea in front shortly after. But the script for this game had already been written. There are just five minutes left on the clock when James Milner volleys the ball back across the box and Lampard's predatory instincts ensure he is first to the ball to put City level.

Understandably, there is no real celebration from the former England man, but the City fans loved it, resulting in shouts of 'Super Frank!' It was enough to earn the Blues a 1-1 draw and a clearly emotional Lampard had the unusual experience of having his name chanted by both sets of fans.

25 November 2014

Trailing 2-1 to Pep Guardiola's ten-man Bayern Munich at the Etihad, City look to be on the way out of the Champions League. But there will be a dramatic climax to the game and it begins five minutes from the end of normal time when Samir Nasri intercepts a sloppy pass from Xabi Alonso and plays it into the path of Sergio Aguero. The City striker drives towards the Bayern box with defenders trailing in his wake before sending a precise, low shot past Manuel Neuer and just inside the left-hand post to make it 2-2 – and set up a thrilling finale in the process.

86

13 May 1989

With a nightmare final-day scenario developing for City, tensions at Valley Parade were at fever pitch as the Blues chased the goal that would mean promotion back to the top flight. Bradford City led 1-0 and, with third-placed Crystal Palace ahead in their last game, City needed an equaliser to confirm promotion. A second goal for the home side and another for Palace would see the London side go up at City's expense but, finally, the goal came with just minutes remaining. Paul Moulden knocked a pass into space on the left and David White managed to beat the defender and cross low into the six-yard box where Trevor Morley slid in to guide the ball home and earn a 1-1 draw that meant promotion for Mel Machin's side.

87

11 August 2001

Stuart Pearce puts the cherry on the cake in Kevin Keegan's first match in charge of City. Leading 2-0 against Watford at Maine Road, the Blues are awarded a free kick on the edge of the box. Pearce, with a fearsome reputation from set pieces, is only ever going to take this and he duly thumps a beauty around the wall and into the top corner to mark his debut with a trademark strike and completes a thoroughly deserved 3-0 win over the Hornets.

29 September 2007

Elano Blumer was one of those players City fans feel they never quite saw enough of. A superb playmaker, capable of driving the Blues to victory when he was at his very best, his two-year stay was all-too brief considering his status among supporters. And it was moments like this, against Newcastle, that made him such an indispensable figure for City fans. At a sun-drenched Etihad Stadium, City, looking to continue their 100 per cent home record under Sven-Goran Eriksson, took on Newcastle United. Elano had been one of seven new signings the Swede had made during the summer and, for many, he was the best. City were leading 2-1 but it wasn't until three minutes from time that Elano had his moment. Sizing up a free kick 30 yards out (at least), the Brazil star runs up and hits a shot that arrows into the top corner to make it 3-1. It was his first goal for the Blues and one of the best free kicks ever seen at the Etihad.

6 February 2016

Too little, too late, as title-chasing Leicester stun the Etihad as they lead 3-0 in a top-of-the-table clash. City's consolation goal is a cracking header worthy of winning any game, as Sergio Aguero rises to meet Bersant Celina's fine cross, heading powerfully past Kasper Schmeichel from a difficult angle to make the score 1-3 in the Foxes' favour – and make a huge dent in City's own faltering title aspirations.

26 February 2020

A huge blow to Real Madrid as their skipper Sergio Ramos makes a cynical challenge on Gabriel Jesus just outside the box. The Brazilian looked set to put City 3-1 up but the skipper decides to 'take one for the team' and is shown a straight red card. Ramos is suspended for the return leg and many believe that eventually sealed Los Blancos' fate in the Champions League for 2019/20.

88

23 March 1988

Surely not! City score a second in the space of four minutes to reduce what had been a deficit of 5-1 to 5-3. Paul Simpson holds the ball on the left and seems to have waited too long as two defenders close in – but the young City winger tricks his way past both of them before whipping in a cross that Chelsea defender Doug Rougvie knocks past his own keeper to – if nothing else – make the score in the Full Members' Cup Final at Wembley look more respectable.

15 May 2005

Possibly the most bizarre substitution in City's history very nearly works. Drawing 1-1 with Middlesbrough at the Etihad, City need to find the winning goal that will secure European football – but with time running out, manager Stuart Pearce decides to roll the dice. He brings Claudio Reyna off and puts on reserve goalkeeper Nicky Weaver – Weaver heads to City's net while David James runs to the sidelines to change his keeper jersey for an outfield shirt bearing the name 'James' and No.1 on the back. James immediately joins the attack and causes havoc every time City attack, and his presence seems to unnerve the Boro defenders as a penalty is awarded for handball in added time. It seems like a fairy-tale end to the game, but Robbie Fowler's poor penalty is easily saved by Mark Schwarzer – the final whistle goes shortly after and the point is enough to ensure it is Middlesbrough and not City who win a UEFA Cup spot.

3 December 2011

No striker quite exuded effortless cool to the same extent as Mario Balotelli and this moment sum up his personality and confidence in his own ability perfectly. Clever link-up play after a darting run from Adam Johnson sends Balotelli clear on goal, but his first strike is smartly saved by Norwich goalkeeper John Ruddy. With Ruddy immobilised from the diving save, the ball loops up into the air and Balotelli calmly follows it towards the goal. While most players would probably choose to head the ball into the empty net, Mario chooses the unique option of shrugging the ball home with his shoulder, sending the Etihad Stadium into suitable reverence. What VAR would have made of it we will never know.

4 October 2014

City had waited 82 minutes to break down Aston Villa's stoic resistance with a Yaya Toure goal – and six minutes later, Sergio Aguero seals the points. James Milner plays the ball to Aguero who controls the pass and nudges it to the right before rifling a powerful shot past Brad Guzan from the edge of the box.

24 May 2015

Sergio Aguero ends the 2014/15 season with his 32nd goal in just 42 starts – an incredible return for a striker who finishes just one behind Golden Boot winner Harry Kane (who played more matches). It is another simple goal for Aguero as Eliaquim Mangala heads the ball across the six-yard box where the unmarked City striker nods into an empty net to complete another stunning season's work.

18 May 2019

Raheem Sterling bags his second of the game to put City 6-0 up in the FA Cup Final against Watford. Bernardo finds Kevin De Bruyne who sends a low cross into the box where Raheem Sterling sweeps a low shot that is touched on to the post by keeper Gomes, but Sterling is quick to snap up the loose ball and complete the Wembley rout that means the Blues are the first side to complete a domestic clean sweep of Premier League, Carabao Cup, Community Shield and FA Cup all in one season – the 'Fourmidables' indeed!

89

4 September 1979

Trailing 1-0 in a League Cup second-round, second-leg tie against Sheffield Wednesday at Maine Road, City find themselves 2-1 down on aggregate after drawing the first leg 1-1. With at best a couple of minutes remaining, midfielder Tony Henry levels for the Blues to seemingly send the game into extra time – but there was still one final twist to come ...

6 December 1981

City wrap up a rare but welcome win at Anfield with a goal a minute from time. Leading 2-1, the Blues keep attacking and Ray Ranson sets Steve Kinsey free on the right flank. The young winger weighs up his options before spotting Kevin Reeves's clever run in front of Phil Thompson, crossing in low and Reeves's clever back-flick is pushed against the foot of the post by Bruce Grobbelaar who then sees the ball rebound against his head and go into the back of the net to seal a 3-1 win for the Blues. An own goal in today's world, but back then, it was Reeves who quite rightly took the credit.

23 March 1988

City make it three goals in five minutes – but still trail 5-4 in a thrilling Full Members' Cup Final at Wembley.

The fourth goal for the Blues – who had trailed 5-1 with 85 minutes on the clock – comes when Andy May works his way into the box only to be brought down by a late tackle and the referee correctly awards a penalty. Mark Lillis wastes no time in drilling a low drive in off the left-hand post to put City on the verge of possibly the greatest comeback of all time, but despite the heroics, the referee allows little or no added time – despite there being seven goals scored in the second half – and Chelsea hold on to win 5-4.

23 October 2011

Dreamland for City who take a 4-1 lead over Manchester United at Old Trafford – and it's thoroughly deserved, too. The goal that sends thousands of home fans flooding towards the exits comes when David Silva's corner is flicked on by Gareth Barry towards the far post. With no United defender in sight, Joleon Lescott keeps the ball in play with a short cross that Edin Dzeko volleys over the line with his knee to seal victory over ten-man United.

6 May 2012

City finally seal three points and move within one win of a first Premier League title in 44 years. Leading 1-0 in a tense game away to Newcastle United, City clear a corner and the ball is won by Sergio Aguero midway inside his own half. He carries it into the Magpies' half before playing it to Nigel de Jong who then quickly plays it his left for Gael Clichy. The left-back sizes up his options before playing a clever short pass to Yaya Toure who takes a touch and fires the ball over Tim Krul to make it 2-0 at St James' Park, sparking wild scenes of celebration among the relieved 3,000 travelling City fans.

4 December 2015

Not perhaps the way Sergio Aguero would have wanted to celebrate his 100th Manchester City goal, but a notable landmark all the same. After leading 1-0 with just eight minutes played, City find themselves 4-1 down to Manchester United at Old Trafford and with just a minute or so remaining. Frank Lampard spots Pablo Zabaleta's run into the box, finds him with a clever pass and his cross finds Aguero on the edge of the six-yard box and City's top scorer makes no mistake, despite David De Gea's best efforts – though it is little more than a consolation.

16 August 2016

Sergio Aguero completes Steaua Bucharest's misery by collecting the ball some 40 yards from goal, powering forward to the edge of the box before unleashing a shot that hits the post and spins into the opposite corner to complete another hat-trick for the Blues and put City 5-0 up in the first leg of the Champions League play-off tie.

90

3 August 1968

City complete the FA Charity Shield rout over West Brom at Maine Road. The sixth and final goal was again partly down to defending that Billy Smart's Circus would be proud of. Alan Oakes feeds Colin Bell on the left and his looping cross finds Mike Summerbee who nods down to Francis Lee. Lee's shot is straight at keeper Merrick who caps a woeful second-half display as he crouches to collect the ball but allows it to somehow evade his grasp and trickle home for number six. Three assists for Buzzer, two goals each for Bobby Owen and Franny Lee and an own goal and a mistake that led to Neil Young's effort – all in all a shambolic 90 minutes of 'defending' by the Baggies who are fortunate to leave with only a 6-1 hiding.

4 September 1979

Having levelled a minute earlier against Sheffield Wednesday, Tony Henry grabs a second goal in two minutes to give City a dramatic 2-1 win over the Owls. The Blues had been on the brink of going out of the League Cup, trailing 2-1 on aggregate with 89 minutes played, but Henry's dramatic brace instead sends City through 3-2 on aggregate.

7 November 1989

The tenth goal of an unforgettable Division Two clash with bottom of the table Huddersfield Town goes to City youth team graduate Andy May – now in the colours of Huddersfield! With his team trailing 9-0 at Maine Road, May steps up to take a consolation penalty for the visitors and, as he emphatically dispatches the spot kick, the City fans cheer the goal and sing May's name which he in turn acknowledges in what had been an otherwise miserable return to his former club.

30 May 1999

As devastated City fans head for the Wembley exits, and the 1999 Division Two (third tier) play-off final looks like ending in defeat to Gillingham, Kevin Horlock gives City a lifeline. With the Gills 2-0 up and seemingly home and hosed, the ball is played through to Shaun Goater who sees his effort blocked as keeper Vince Bartram races out, but the clearance only goes as far as Kevin Horlock who hits a crisp low shot from the edge of the box and into the net to halve the deficit with just five minutes of added time to play. For many, it's no more than a consolation but there is still time for what would be one of Wembley's most dramatic comebacks ever ...

23 August 2003

In the first ever Premier League game at the City of Manchester Stadium (renamed the Etihad, of course, in later years), City toil without reward and trail Portsmouth

1-0. Just when the visitors seem certain to spoil the party as the game goes into injury time, City are awarded a free kick. The Blues send virtually everyone bar David James into the box and as Joey Barton's cross comes in, French defender David Sommeil leaps highest to nod the ball past Shaka Hislop and become the Blues' first Premier League scorer at the new Eastlands home. The game ends 1-1 and Sommeil assures his place in the club's history books.

4 February 2004

With the clock ticking towards 90 minutes, ten-man City press for an unlikely winner in the FA Cup replay with Spurs at White Hart Lane. Having trailed 3-0 at the break, extra time would surely favour the home team, with a chance to regroup and restore sanity. It was now or never as the Blues conjured up one last attack. The ball is deep in the Spurs half when it finds its way to Michael Tarnat. The cultured German left-back looks up and sends a deep cross towards the back post where Jon Macken – still with an awful lot to do – connects perfectly with his head and then watches as the ball sails past Kasey Keller and into the net – cue pandemonium. The City fans, players and management go wild and the Tottenham players look at each other in total disbelief. Three goals up, 45 minutes to play and the opposition down to ten men. They'd blown it and the final whistle goes moments later, completing one of the greatest comebacks of all time and one of the most exciting FA

Cup matches ever. As Kevin Keegan succinctly points out afterwards, 'They'll be talking about this match long after we've all gone.' He wasn't wrong!

14 March 2004

Any goal scored in a Manchester derby is special for the player concerned and the supporters who can celebrate it, but Shaun Wright-Phillips's stunning strike against Manchester United in the 2003/04 derby was something to cherish. City were already 3-1 up when, with just a few minutes remaining, Shaun Wright-Phillips chased a ball that ran along the right touchline for about 12 feet – but stayed in play. He then cut in towards the United box with Reds defender Wes Brown ahead of him and no other option – he touches the ball to the right before hammering a shot that hits the underside of the bar which then bounces down and into the net giving Tim Howard no chance. Just as City had won the last derby at Maine Road the previous season, so the Blues win the first derby at the City of Manchester Stadium in style.

9 April 2005

Kiki Musampa, on loan from Atletico Madrid, had already gone close with a shot that hit the post, while Liverpool offered little in the way of a threat. As the clock ticked past 90 minutes, it seemed neither side would find the back of the net in what had still been an entertaining enough encounter. Then, Lee Croft finds space on the right flank but, instead of driving a cross into the box, he spots Musampa approaching the edge of the box and dinks a pass to the former Ajax man who skips towards the ball and volleys a low shot that gives Liverpool keeper Scott Carson no chance. The City fans go wild – a win over Liverpool was rare to say the least at that time – and the Blues hold firm to win 1-0, helping Pearce secure the manager's job on a permanent basis.

2 March 2014

City win possession in their own half as Sunderland desperately search for a late equaliser, but the gamble backfires as City break with five against two. Yaya Toure powers through the middle before playing an inviting ball into the path of Jesus Navas who sees his low shot squeeze under the keeper to put City 3-1 up and seal a Capital Cup triumph for Manuel Pellegrini – his first trophy in England.

30 September 2015

Yet another successful penalty from Sergio Aguero. It is Aguero who is fouled in the box and converts the spot kick himself with a low shot into the bottom right-hand corner to give City a last-gasp 2-1 win away to Borussia Monchengladbach in a Champions League group-stage clash in Germany.

90+1

15 August 2011

What a way to start your life in sky blue. Already with a goal and an assist, Sergio Aguero collects the ball midway into the Swansea half and with little else on and time running out, he unleashes a sublime 25-yard shot that gives Swansea keeper Michel Vorm no chance and completes a 4-0 victory for City. Two goals and an assist in just 33 minutes or so of first-team football for City – and he was in pain with blisters on his feet at the time, hence only being named a sub. The City fans had a new hero, but it was only the beginning ...

23 October 2011

A swift counter-attack sees City increase the lead over Manchester United to 5-1 at Old Trafford. Edin Dzeko receives the ball just inside the Reds' half before nutmegging a United defender to set David Silva clear on the right of the box – the brilliant Spaniard controls the pass before opening up his body and sending a low shot under his Spanish international team-mate David De Gea to get the goal his superb all-round display deserved – but neither Silva nor City were quite finished ...

25 November 2014

A famous Champions League night at the Etihad sees City snatch victory from the jaws of defeat against ten-man Bayern Munich. What proves to be the game's decisive goal comes when former City player Jerome Boateng gives possession away outside his own box, enabling Sergio Aguero to steal the ball and dash into the Bayern Munich box. As three Bayern defenders close in, Aguero places a low shot past the keeper to complete a superb hat-trick and give City a dramatic 3-2 win over Pep Guardiola's side.

14 September 2016

Kelechi Iheanacho completes a comprehensive victory over Borussia Monchengladbach in the Champions League group-stage clash at the Etihad. Already leading 3-0 thanks to a Sergio Aguero hat-trick, City wrap up the points as Leroy Sane spots the young striker in the centre of the box, crosses low and Iheanacho plants the ball home from 12 yards out.

1 March 2017

Kelechi Iheanacho scores with the last kick of the game to seal a 5-1 FA Cup fifth-round replay victory over Huddersfield Town. The Nigerian, who had only been on the pitch 12 minutes after replacing two-goal Sergio Aguero from the bench, is on hand to finish Jesus Navas's cross from close range.

9 September 2017

Leroy Sane puts the icing on the cake as City complete their thrashing of title rivals Liverpool at the Etihad. Sane bags his second when he collects a pass from Kyle Walker before cutting in from the left and curling a beauty from 20 yards into the top-left corner to make it 5-0 over ten-man Liverpool.

90+2

7 November 1987

With the City fans baying for a tenth goal but time almost up, Huddersfield Town's beleaguered keeper hits a long kick downfield in the hope the referee will surely end his and his team-mates' misery. But City win possession and, as the ball is played into the path of David White, the electric-paced forward bursts clear on goal and takes it around the goalkeeper, before planting an angled shot past a despairing defender's desperate lunge to complete his hat-trick and put City 10-1 up and send Maine Road wild with delight. Remarkably, White's hat-trick is the third of the game, with Tony Adcock and Paul Stewart also both scoring trebles. A very special afternoon for those there to witness it in the flesh.

13 May 2012

As the City fans watch in despair as the title seemingly slips away, Edin Dzeko provides a lifeline. Trailing 2-1 to QPR and needing a win to seal a first Premier League triumph and first top-flight title for 44 years, City win a corner on the right. David Silva whips the ball into the six-yard box where an unmarked Dzeko heads down and past Paddy Kenny to make it 2-2 with just a couple of minutes of added time remaining.

23 November 2013

Jesus Navas caps a superb display by finishing what he had started against Tottenham. The livewire winger had put City on the way with a goal after just 14 seconds and he bookends a brilliant City performance as he races clear onto James Milner's through ball before tucking a low drive past Hugo Lloris to make it 6-0 at a jubilant Etihad Stadium.

29 January 2014

Sergio Aguero completes a superb hat-trick against Watford to single-handedly put City into the next round of the FA Cup. Having already bagged the goals that brought City level, the Argentina star rises to head home Jesus Navas's looping cross and finally kill off a spirited Watford's hopes of a shock win at the Etihad.

17 August 2014

City are leading 1-0 at St James' Park but the hosts are still in the game and in with a shout of taking a point until Sergio Aguero picks up the ball midway through the Newcastle half, heads into the box, drifting past compatriot Fabricio Coloccini in the process before firing a left-foot shot at Tim Krul. The Newcastle keeper saves the attempt but Aguero is first to the rebound and curls home right-footed from the corner of the six-yard box to seal a 2-0 win for the defending champions.

90+3

29 December 2001

Sub Darren Huckerby puts the icing on the cake as City complete a 5-1 thrashing of Division One leaders Burnley at Maine Road. Huckerby, on for Shaun Goater, races half the length of the field to beat Nick Michopoulos for the fifth home goal of the afternoon as City narrow the gap to the Clarets to just one point in the race for a Premier League return under Kevin Keegan.

90+4

19 February 2006

City's FA Cup dream appears to be over at Villa Park. Trailing to Milan Baros's effort, Stuart Pearce's side seemed to be having 'one of those nights' when nothing would go their way. So when the board went up for four minutes of injury time, hopes of salvation were slim. With time almost up, Lee Croft wins a corner and City have one last chance. Croft swings the ball in and goalkeeper David James, who'd joined the final attack, leaps up, misses, but behind him and leaping even higher is 17-year-old defender Micah Richards who powers a header past Thomas Sorensen and into the net for the most dramatic of equalisers – and to earn City a replay.

24 November 2007

A last-gasp goal to savour. City were desperate to continue the home form that had seen them win every home game going into late November. Up against a determined and focused Reading side, the Blues finally break the deadlock when Martin Petrov scores for City, but the Royals hit back before the break when James Harper curls in an equaliser to send the teams in level. The second half was mostly City knocking on the door with Reading hanging on and as the game drifted into injury time, it seemed Steve Coppell's side would take what had seemed like an unlikely point. Then, with 94 minutes played and the visiting fans pleading with the referee to call time, the Blues launch one final attack as Vedran Corluka plays the ball up to Georgios Samaras whose header is then nodded on by Geovanni into the path of Stephen Ireland who strikes a sweet volley home from 18 yards that rockets into the roof of the net to send the Etihad Stadium wild and seal a 2-1 win

28 August 2011

Edin Dzeko completes a memorable afternoon in North London as he bags his fourth of the game to complete a 5-1 win over Tottenham. The icing on the cake comes when Dzeko exchanges passes with Gareth Barry who prods the ball into the Bosnian's path and Dzeko fires a superb curling left-foot shot into the top-left corner to give the keeper no chance as City send a warning to the rest of the Premier League that they are going to take some stopping in 2011/12.

20 October 2011

With City being held at home to Villarreal in the Champions League and time running out, the Blues launch one last, hopeful attack. Pablo Zabaleta crosses low into the six-yard box and David Silva's extravagant back-flick sees the ball head towards the far post where Aguero lunges just ahead of Dzeko to bundle the ball over the line for a dramatic, last-gasp winner and reignite City's Champions League campaign in dramatic style.

23 October 2011

Arguably the best goal of the game sends City fans into ecstasy at Old Trafford as the Blues score a third in the space of five minutes to complete an historic and record-equalling 6-1 win over Manchester United. A long punt is headed clear by the United defence, but only as far as David Silva on the halfway line who cushions the ball up on his right foot as it comes to him and then half-volleys an inch-perfect pass into the path of Edin Dzeko who doesn't even have to break his stride before powering home his second and City's sixth at the now near-empty stadium – bar the 3,000 disbelieving City fans in the corner.

5 March 2012

With the Blues needing one more goal to seal a place in the Europa League quarter-finals, the proverbial kitchen sink was thrown at the Sporting Lisbon defence. Two near-miss headers from Edin Dzeko and Mario Balotelli were just the preparation for the drama which was still to come. A corner deep into stoppage time presents Joe Hart with the chance of a rare venture into the opposition's box, and he remains there until the end of the game. Hearts are in mouths as England's No.1 throws himself on to the end of a Nigel de Jong cross, executing a perfect header in the direction of the bottom corner – only for a fantastic reaction save from his opposite number Rui Patricio in the Sporting goal who diverts the ball round the far post. The referee blows for full time immediately after, not allowing time for the resulting corner.

13 May 2012

It is a game and a goal etched in the memory of every City fan and, it's fair to say, every football fan up and down the land. The drama could not have been greater and when people talk of the best games the Premier League has ever produced, the match between Manchester City and QPR is hard to top. The scenario was simple: if City won, they were champions. QPR needed a result to guarantee safety, adding yet more spice to a game that had already reached almost unbearable tension levels for City fans. Surely the Blues, imperious at home all season, would see off struggling QPR and the contest would be all over long before full time? Not quite ... The game ebbed and flowed with nerves frayed but at last, Pablo Zabaleta put City ahead just before the break. It was the second half, however, where everything started to unravel for Roberto Mancini's side. QPR levelled within three minutes of the restart through Djibril Cisse but then an altercation between Joey Barton and Sergio Aguero saw the former City midfielder shown a straight red card. Yet it was QPR who scored next with Jamie Mackie heading home on 66 minutes to give ten-man Rangers a 2-1 lead. With 90 minutes played, the Blues

– incredibly – looked to have blown it. But Aguero's place in history awaited. Edin Dzeko nodded the Blues level in the 92nd minute of the game, and a further two minutes passed when Nigel de Jong made one last foray forward, played the ball to Aguero who found Mario Balotelli and the Italian held off his challenger long enough to slide the ball back into the Argentine's path as he skipped past one challenge and hammered the ball home to win the game with 93 minutes and 20 seconds on the clock. The Etihad Stadium went wild and, as Aguero wheeled away waving his shirt over his head, realisation sank in that City were about to win the Premier League title. It was the most incredible finish imaginable to a Premier League season and the most important goal in the club's 118-year history.

7 May 2014

Just as City had done when hunting down Manchester United's eight-point lead in 2011/12, the Blues had eaten away Liverpool's eight-point advantage to the point the Merseysiders had seemingly cracked under the pressure. With a game in hand, City could finally overtake the Reds in the penultimate game with Aston Villa the visitors for a rearranged game. It was always going to be a tense night, even though Manuel Pellegrini's men were odds-on favourites to win and, though Villa had held out for more than an hour, City ground down the Midlands side and were 3-0 up by the time Yaya Toure picks up the ball in his own half and powers his way forward as perhaps only he could. His momentum takes him past five chasing Villa players who are powerless to stop him and he finishes with a powerful drive from inside the box that send the home fans wild and seals a 4-0 win.

17 April 2019

When you think about it, quite a lot has happened to City in the fourth minute of added time – and while most events were joyous, this one is torturous. Leading 4-3 but about to be eliminated from the Champions League at the quarter-final stage on away goals, the Etihad Stadium goes crazy as Sergio Aguero races into the Tottenham box, squares the ball to Raheem Sterling who sweeps a low shot home to seemingly put City into the semi-final with virtually the last kick of the game. The celebrations are wild and last a while, until the sudden realisation that a VAR review is under way – and within seconds the big screen displays – 'VAR check complete – no goal. Offside'. The Tottenham fans instead begin to celebrate and the final whistle goes soon after, sending the North London side into the semis.

90+5

30 May 1999

As added time ticked down to the final few seconds and City still trailed 2-1 in the 1998/99 play-off final with Gillingham, the Blues try one last, desperate attack. As a long ball is pumped forward, Gareth Taylor flicks the ball into the path of Shaun Goater whose attempt from the edge of the box is blocked, but the loose ball goes to the right and Paul Dickov takes one touch before unleashing a powerful shot past Vince Bartram in goal to make it 2-2 and send the game into extra time. It is a remarkable comeback by the Blues who had trailed 2-0 with 90 minutes played and the goal leads to wild celebrations among the 40,000 City fans inside Wembley.

90+6

29 November 2017

Raheem Sterling scores another last-gasp winner to ensure City's winning run continues. Southampton had proved dogged opponents and, with the score at 1-1, were desperate for the referee to blow for full time, but as the Blues tried one last attack, Sterling delivers yet again. Kevin De Bruyne pokes it to Sterling on the edge of the Saints box and after stopping the ball, he then sends a measured, curling shot into the top-right corner to secure a 2-1 win and send the Etihad Stadium wild with delight.

90+7

8 January 1988

With City leading 1-0 in the FA Cup third-round tie away to Huddersfield, the hosts came out in the second half like scalded cats and, in the space of five minutes, had gone 2-1 up thanks to a Duncan Shearer brace. Having lost 10-1 at Maine Road just eight weeks before, this was payback time for the West Yorkshire side and the Blues' large away following seemingly had to grin and bear it. With 90 minutes up and no boards to indicate how long was left, it looked as though City were out at the first hurdle, but the referee didn't blow and with an incredible seven minutes of injury time played, City won a free kick on the edge of Huddersfield's box. It was the last chance and everyone knew it. Full-back John Gidman – who had never scored for the Blues – steps up, curls the ball around the wall from 20 yards out and into the back of the net. The City fans go wild and dance around Leeds Road's wide terraces for several minutes as a 2-2 draw and a replay is secured with the last kick of the game.

26 August 2017

Raheem Sterling grabs a dramatic stoppage-time winner to give City a 2-1 victory away to Bournemouth. The Cherries thought they'd done enough to earn a rare point against the Blues when they are forced to defend what seems to be a final attack. Danilo fires in a cross from the right and Sterling takes one touch before spinning and hitting a shot which loops up off a defender and into the opposite corner to seal three points for Pep Guardiola's side.

90+9

26 August 2017

After celebrating that dramatic last-gasp winner at the Vitality Stadium, referee Mike Dean gives Raheem Sterling a second yellow card for his understandable reaction to scoring such an important goal and the City forward – booked earlier in the game – is sent off as a result, confounding the player, City fans and manager as well as taking the gloss off a 2-1 victory over Bournemouth.

90+16

7 January 1978

One of the longest periods of stoppage time ends as City cling on to a 2-1 FA Cup third-round win at Elland Road. The additional time is mostly down to a pitch invasion from Leeds United supporters with crowd trouble dogging the match all afternoon. The referee refuses to abandon the game and, eventually, the crowd is dispersed. Leeds pull one back after the resumption but the Blues deservedly see the game out and move into the next round.

Extra time

92

11 September 2001

Paul Dickov edges City ahead in the League Cup tie with Notts County at Meadow Lane. The Blues had led, then trailed 2-1 in normal time, before Shaun Goater levelled late on to force extra time. Dickov scores a couple of minutes in to put the Blues 3-2 up against the Magpies.

95

21 September 2005

Darius Vassell finally gives City the lead against third-tier side Doncaster Rovers in the League Cup tie at Belle Vue. The hosts had held City 0-0 in normal time, but when the Blues finally break the deadlock, it looks as though City will triumph. But a Nedum Onuoha sending-off on 106 minutes and a Doncaster equaliser on 118 minutes forces a penalty shoot-out that the Blues lose 3-0.

100

11 April 1981

City and Ipswich Town had played out 90 minutes of the FA Cup semi-final at Villa Park and couldn't be separated. The game went into 30 minutes of extra time and with the scores still locked at 0-0, one goal seemed likely to settle the tie. City were attacking the Holte End for the first period of extra time and, with exactly 100 minutes on the clock, were awarded a free kick on the edge of the Ipswich box. Skipper Paul Power, who had scored in every round but one, sized up the defensive wall and Steve Mackenzie rolled the ball gently into his path. The crowd held its breath as he whipped a curling shot towards the goal. Cooper scrambled across to his right as the ball sailed into the top left-hand corner of the net. Half the ground erupted and the blue masses behind the goal went wild. City were on their way to the FA Cup Final for the first time since 1969 with a wonderful goal scored in the 100th minute of the 100th year of FA Cup football – a fitting tribute to the world's oldest tournament.

102

7 March 1970

Despite the sapping Wembley pitch and the tiring redirected journey from Portugal where City had played a midweek European Cup Winners' Cup tie, even the additional extra time couldn't keep this never-say-die City side down. After drawing 1-1 in normal time, and when the watching nation may well have expected West Brom to finish the job off with their fresher legs, the Blues conjure up a 102nd-minute winner. Francis Lee chips a ball to Colin Bell and his back-heel falls perfectly for Glyn Pardoe. The left-back looks up and squeezes a drive past the Baggies keeper from the corner of the box for a dramatic winner. There were no further goals and Tony Book lifted the League Cup for the first time in the club's history.

103

11 September 2001

Darren Huckerby finally ends Notts County's resistance in the League Cup tie at Meadow Lane. The City winger scores the Blues' second extra-time goal to seal a 4-2 win over the Magpies and book a next-round tie at home to Birmingham City.

105

23 April 2017

Kelechi Iheanacho becomes City's first ever fourth substitute as he replaces Raheem Sterling in the FA Cup semi-final against Arsenal. City are 2-1 down to the Gunners at the time and there will be no more goals as the Gunners triumph at Wembley.

108

24 September 2008

Stephen Ireland equalises against Brighton in the League Cup second-round tie at the Withdean Stadium. City had led 1-0 up until the 89th minute when Glenn Murray levelled for the Seagulls, forcing extra time. The hosts then take a 2-1 lead through Joseph Anyinsah before Ireland levels to make it 2-2. However, the Blues are beaten 5-3 on penalties by the League One side.

111

23 September 2009

Kolo Toure finally settles the League Cup tie with Fulham after the visitors had forced extra time. Toure heads Martin Petrov's corner home from about a yard to give City a 2-1 lead and, with no further scoring, to book a place in the last 16 of the competition.

Penalty shoot-outs

City have a decent record in penalty shoot-outs – here are some of the memorable ones:

30 May 1999

After the play-off final with Gillingham failed to produce any more goals in extra time, the match ended 2-2 and went to a penalty shoot-out at Wembley.

Here's how the shoot-out prevailed ...

- Kevin Horlock (Manchester City) – scores – 1-0
- Paul Smith (Gillingham) – misses – 1-0
- Paul Dickov (Manchester City) – misses – 1-0
- Adrian Pennock (Gillingham) – misses – 1-0
- Terry Cooke (Manchester City) – scores – 2-0
- John Hodge (Gillingham) – scores – 2-1
- Richard Edghill (Manchester City) – scores – 3-1
- Guy Butters (Gillingham) – misses – 3-1

Manchester City win 3-1 on penalties.

28 February 2016

City and Liverpool end the 2016 Carabao Cup Final level at 1-1 after extra time and the match at Wembley goes to a penalty shoot-out – here's how it panned out ...

- Emre Can (Liverpool) – scores – 1-0
- Fernandinho (Manchester City) – misses – 1-0
- Lucas Leiva (Liverpool) – misses – 1-0
- Jesus Navas (Manchester City) – scores – 1-1
- Philippe Coutinho (Liverpool) misses – 1-1
- Sergio Aguero (Manchester City) – scores – 1-2
- Adam Lallana (Liverpool) – misses – 1-2
- Yaya Toure (Manchester City) – scores – 1-3

Manchester City win 3-1 on penalties

25 October 2017

City are held by enterprising Championship side Wolves in the Carabao Cup fourth round at the Etihad. The teams end normal time 0-0 and there are no goals in extra time, resulting in a penalty shoot-out. Here's what happened ... This is the first time City have been involved in an ABBA system shoot-out – where, after the first spot kick, both sides take two penalties consecutively.

- Leo Bonatini (Wolves) – scores – 1-0
- Yaya Toure (Manchester City) – scores – 1-1
- Kevin De Bruyne (Manchester City) – scores – 1-2

- Alfred N'Diaye (Wolves) – misses – 1-2
- Conor Coady (Wolves) – misses – 1-2
- Leroy Sane (Manchester City) – scores – 1-3
- Sergio Aguero (Manchester City) – scores – 1-4

Manchester City win 4-1 on penalties

19 December 2017

Leicester and City draw 1-1 in normal time at the King Power Stadium and, when extra time cannot separate the sides, a penalty shoot-out ensues for a place in the Carabao Cup semi-finals.

The ABBA system is once again used...

- Christian Fuchs (Leicester City) – scores – 1-0
- Ilkay Gundogan (Manchester City) – scores – 1-1
- Yaya Toure (Manchester City) – scores – 1-2
- Harry Maguire (Leicester City) – scores – 2-2
- Vicente Iborra (Leicester City) – scores – 3-2
- Lukas Nmecha (Manchester City) – scores – 3-3
- Gabriel Jesus (Manchester City) – scores – 3-4
- Jamie Vardy (Leicester City) – misses – 3-4
- Riyad Mahrez (Leicester City) – misses – 3-4

Manchester City win 4-3 on penalties

18 December 2018

Leicester and City draw 1-1 in normal time and, when extra time cannot separate the sides, a penalty shoot-out ensues for a place in the Carabao Cup semi-finals.

- Harry Maguire (Leicester City) – scores – 1-0
- Ilkay Gundogan (Manchester City) – scores – 1-1
- Christian Fuchs (Leicester City) – misses – 1-1
- Raheem Sterling (Manchester City) – misses – 1-1
- James Maddison (Leicester City) – misses – 1-1
- Gabriel Jesus (Manchester City) – scores – 1-2
- Caglar Söyüncü (Leicester City) – misses – 1-2
- Oleksandr Zinchenko (Manchester City) – scores – 1-3

Manchester City win 3-1 on penalties

24 February 2019

City and Chelsea couldn't be separated in normal or extra time with the 2019 Carabao Cup Final ending 0-0 and going to a penalty shoot-out at Wembley.

Here's how it panned out ...

- Jorginho (Chelsea) – misses – 0-0
- Ilkay Gundogan (Manchester City) – scores – 0-1
- Cesar Azpilicueta (Chelsea) – scores – 1-1
- Sergio Aguero (Manchester City) – scores – 1-2

- Emerson (Chelsea) – scores – 2-2
- Leroy Sane (Manchester City) – misses – 2-2
- David Luiz (Chelsea) – misses – 2-2
- Bernardo Silva (Manchester City) – scores – 2-3
- Eden Hazard (Chelsea) – scores – 3-3
- Raheem Sterling (Manchester City) – scores – 3-4

Manchester City win 4-3 on penalties

4 August 2019

City and Liverpool cannot be separated in the 2019 FA Community Shield at Wembley after drawing 1-1 in normal time. The match went straight to penalties and, just three years earlier, City beat Liverpool 3-1 in penalties to secure the Carabao Cup – here's what happened on this occasion ...

- Xherdan Shaqiri (Liverpool) – scores – 1-0
- Ilkay Gundogan (Manchester City) – scores – 1-1
- Georginio Wijnaldum (Liverpool) – misses – 1-1
- Bernardo Silva (Manchester City) – scores – 1-2
- Adam Lallana (Liverpool) – scores – 2-2
- Phil Foden (Manchester City) – scores – 2-3
- Alex Oxlade-Chamberlain (Liverpool) – scores – 3-3
- Oleksandr Zinchenko (Manchester City) – scores – 3-4

- Mo Salah (Liverpool) – scores – 4-4
- Gabriel Jesus (Manchester City) – scores – 4-5

Manchester City win 5-4 on penalties

Also available at all good book stores

9781909178717

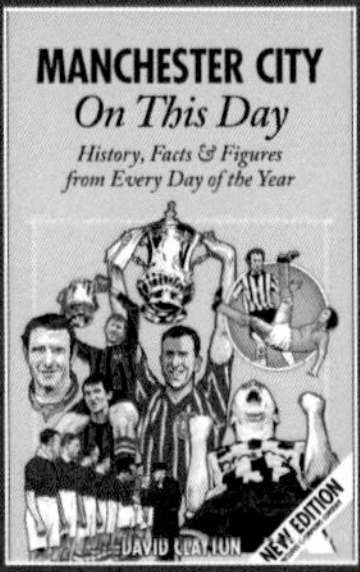

9781908051004

9781785314384

9781785314995

9781785315381

9781785315411

9781785315312

9781785315060

9781785315237